1 - The Lamp of Life Renewed

The LAMP OF LIFE Renewed

The
LAMP OF LIFE
Renewed

DAILY MEDITATIONS FOR THE EASTER SEASON

Rev. ROGER A. SWENSON

ALBA · HOUSE   NEW · YORK

SOCIETY OF ST. PAUL, 2187 VICTORY BLVD., STATEN ISLAND, NEW YORK 10314

Scripture quotations
are from the
New American Bible
Confraternity of Christian Doctrine,
©1969, 1970.

Library of Congress Cataloging-in-Publication Data

Swenson, Roger A.
  The lamp of life renewed: daily meditations for the Easter season
  /by Roger A. Swenson.
    p. 155   14 x 21 cm.
  ISBN 0-8189-0534-4
  1. Eastertide — Prayer-books and devotions — English.   I. Title.
BX2170.E25S94   1988   88-10480
242'.36 — dc 19   CIP

Nihil Obstat:
Rev. Msgr. Henry C. Bezou
Censor Librorum

Imprimatur:
† Most Rev. Philip M. Hannan
Archbishop of New Orleans
January 19, 1988

Designed, printed and bound in the United States of
America by the Fathers and Brothers of the
Society of St. Paul, 2187 Victory Boulevard,
Staten Island, New York 10314, as part of their
communications apostolate.

© *Copyright 1988 by the Society of St. Paul*

Printing Information:

Current Printing - first digit 1 2 3 4 5 6 7 8 9 10 11 12 13 14 15 16 17 18 19 20

Year of Current Printing - first year shown
           1988 1989 1990 1991 1992 1993 1994 1995 1996 1997 1998 1999 2000 2001 2002

to
LARRY HECKER

FOREWORD

The II Vatican Council has stated in its most solemn document, Lumen Gentium, that "everyone in the Church does not proceed by the same path, nevertheless all are called to sanctity and have received an equal privilege of faith through the justice of God (cf. 2 Peter 1:1). And if by the will of Christ some are made teachers, dispensers of mysteries, and shepherds on behalf of others, yet all share a true equality with regard to the dignity and activity common to all the faithful for the building up of the Body of Christ" (n. 32).

This excellent book of meditations, *The Lamp of Life Renewed* is a faithful guide in showing each of us how to build up the Body of Christ in our lives. The renewal of our lives is a steady, daily effort which centers very largely on our immediate duties and concerns. As our physical growth depends upon a slow but constant process, so our spiritual depends upon a persevering process that makes each day and each week a contribution to the life of the spirit.

During his visit to the United States in September, 1987, the Holy Father repeatedly stressed the need for daily commitment to Christ. In his address to representatives of the laity in San Francisco, he proclaimed, "It is within the everyday world that you the laity must bear witness to God's kingdom.... You are called to live in the world, to engage in secular professions and occupations, to live in those ordinary circumstances of family life and life in society from which is woven the very web of your existence."

A study of the life of Christ on earth reveals His attention to the daily cares and familial concerns of the people. He dealt with a crisis in a wedding feast, curing the servant of a centurion, caring for the physical needs of the thousands who came to hear Him. His public ministry was the capstone of many years of quiet family life in a little village where He, His mother and foster-father must have been involved in the daily needs of their neighbors. The message of Jesus, in all His ministry, was the value of the interior spiritual development of every person and their nurturing that development by their service to others in daily living.

The meditations in this book radiate from Easter, the triumph of life over death. Using these meditations will enable us to participate in the life of Christ according to those splendid words of St. Peter read in the Liturgy of Easter, "When Christ your life appears, you too will appear with Him in glory" (Colossians 3:4).

† Philip M. Hannan
Archbishop of New Orleans
January 12, 1988

INTRODUCTION

"It was now around midday, and darkness came over the whole land until midafternoon with an eclipse of the sun" (Luke 23:44). In the heart of an itinerant preacher from Galilee, the light of the world was going out. At this bleakest of all of history's hours, no other source of warmth or illumination would be permitted to offer even a spark of hope. There would be no mitigation of the darkness of this tragedy. In obedience to the Father of light who allowed the night of death to fall upon his Son, the sun itself would abdicate its throne. On that Friday of catcalls and cowardice, the shadow line swept across the land and through the city. Birds folded their wings and fell silent, cattle lay down to early slumber, men and women in the streets recoiled against dusty walls at the premature onset of dusk and invoked not Yahweh but the proscribed gods of Canaan. The edge of night moved swiftly up the puny slope of Golgotha, struck the bottom of the upright pole, was not checked. No god, no power could stop the advance of this swelling shade as it engulfed bloody feet, heaving chest, imploring arms, and then at last, in triumph shrouded the lolling head. The color of chaos, the darkness of Genesis, had won.

On May 30, 1984, most Americans went about their business with earth-anchored determination. The brief twilight in the late morning was to many merely a sign of impending rain. Sky-watchers knew better; they fled from the smog of cities to cloudless vistas, taking with them the baggage of the amateur astronomer. For their trouble, they were rewarded with a diamond ring. The diamond ring effect is the phenomenon which takes place at the central moment of a total eclipse of the sun. For a split second, all is dark; suddenly the first spark of the newborn sun glimmers, then explodes in radiance, becoming a gleaming diamond at the edge of the unseen moon. It spends itself briefly as the remainder of the sun is uncovered in a thickening corona of fire. That diamond, that pure, white incandescence is the promise that the sun will shine whole and entire again, that birds will fly and cattle will forage and men and women will walk determinedly in the streets once more. That blaze of glory is the symbol of this book. It is the first glimpse of the lamp of life renewed.

One by one, the fifty days of Easter proclaim that the eclipse which chilled Jerusalem on that long-ago Friday afternoon was not the death of God's love for humankind. Although God's beloved died on the Hill of the Skull and no compensating light would bathe the earth in that hour, that hour was not to be the last. Thirty-six more and the Risen Christ would prove that while God's love could be eclipsed by pride and fear, it could not be extinguished. There would be a diamond in a ring of promise casting a beam powerful enough to split rocks, to dazzle soldiers, to warm frightened hearts. Only a few would dare to believe what they saw at the empty tomb, at the Sea of Tiberias, or on the road to Emmaus. No matter how incredible it seemed, however, the light had been reborn; its warmth and luster would become more convincing with time. The Church symbolizes this period of enlightenment in the seven weeks of Easter.

The following meditations will lead the reader to appreciate more the teaching of Jesus which preceded the eclipse of God's love on the first Good Friday. This process of discernment will be enhanced by a prayerful examination of the Gospel according to John against the reflected glory of the Resurrection. From time to time, the stories of the first Christians as reported in the Acts of the Apostles will be used to show how the light grew brighter, guiding the disciples and their converts through the wonders of the Ascension and Pentecost and beyond. Beyond are Peter's visions and Paul's journey's. Beyond is also today.

This book is written for today, for and about men and women of faith who sometimes wonder if the light which once led them has dimmed. It is not uncommon to feel the need to compromise, to give in to the encroaching darkness of materialism and amorality. Nor is it unnatural to be tempted by hazy interpretations of Biblical truths and Church teachings. Let the reader be warned: There is no compromise in these pages. The glory has not faded, but the lamp of life renewed produces heat as well as light. The flash of long-avoided truth can sear the soul. Many of these meditations require the courage to expose one's way of life to the purifying flame. This is not a cool book.

As the warm sun of springtime draws forth from the fertile earth the first stirrings of new life, so the light of the Risen Christ reflected in these pages is meant to draw from John's Gospel and the Acts of the Apostles new insights for daily living. The task of the reader is to tend the fragile growth. This spiritual husbandry requires a daily intention to find a quiet place of prayer and to set aside fifteen minutes for communion with the Lord. Neither aim is easily accomplished in this busy world, but not the sun nor the Evangelists nor God himself can call forth spiritual growth without the nurturing atmosphere which only the quiet of meditation affords. The place, the time, the purpose is the responsibility of the Christian who searches the mystery of

Christ. Those fortunate to have more time will want to turn to the daily readings of the Masses of the Easter Season to find the complete passages from which the quotations contained herein have been taken.

The mentor for this journey from Easter to Pentecost, from wonder to enlightenment, is the Holy Spirit of Truth to whose urgings St. John and St. Luke conformed their skills. If allowed to do so, this same Spirit will breathe upon the expectant soul, nourishing the springtime growth of consolation, discernment, peace, and zeal. As the first fragile shoots of what would become the universal Church were strengthened and inspired by the Paraclete, so in this day recollected hearts will be encouraged to quicken and expand in love of neighbor and stranger. A new season begins, the season of the soul's maturing. A new people has been born; now they ripen in the warmth of the Sun of Love.

> Whatever came to be in him, found life,
> life for the light of men.
> The light shines on in the darkness,
> a darkness that did not overcome it (John 1:4-5).

DAILY MEDITATIONS FOR THE EASTER SEASON

EASTER SUNDAY

> Early in the morning on the first day of the week, while it was still dark, Mary Magdalene came to the tomb. She saw that the stone had been moved away, so she ran off to Simon Peter and the other disciple [the one Jesus loved] and told them, "The Lord has been taken from the tomb! We don't know where they have put him!"   (John 20:1-2)

The Gospel writers pulled no punches when it came to enumerating the horrors that rained upon the fragile flesh of Jesus in the hours before his death. Our imaginations fill in the details: the crack of a slap in the face, the bitter staccato of spittle, the rip and tear of skin unused to the whip, the rat-a-tat of invective so hateful it seared the air. For their exhaustive presentations of the Lord's final struggle, the Evangelists had various motives: an indictment of the ruling class, a witness to the example of Jesus' suffering, a paean to his personal power towering over the petty stratagems of his accusers. These themes, however, took second place to the principal conclusion of each passion narrative, that is, that no human being, not even the God-man, could have survived the physical and psychological torture which Jesus accepted. In short, he died. He didn't fall into a coma. He didn't pretend to grow cold and rigid. He wasn't offering an object lesson or dramatizing a teachable moment. He lost his life. The holy authors took us step-by-step along the Way of the Cross so they could say with absolute credibility that Jesus "gave up his spirit" (Matthew), "breathed his last" (Mark), "expired" (Luke), "delivered over his spirit" (John). Jesus died.

Last week, we were both fascinated and repelled by the excruciatingly vivid details of Christ's last agony. Today, we are surprised by vagueness. The blow-by-blow account is brought to a close by an antic Sunday morning featuring a man robed in white and another mistaken for a gardener. We stumble in the misty dawn over a limp winding cloth, and back into a huge stone with mud on the top. There are alarums and excursions, women with the vapors, men racing each other and their doubts. The dialogue is as hazy as the morning fog: Where is the body? Did you get the soldiers' statements? You say "dazzling garments"?

This is the way the world begins, not with a history, but a vortex of sensations whirling too swiftly to focus the mind. Matthew, Mark, Luke, and John were more human, more accessible in their broad-brush brevity than the saintly scholars who spend their lives dicing up the Resurrection. It happened like this, the holy writers tell us. Jesus, the long-awaited Savior, had the life crushed out of him. He died and was buried. Forty hours later, his tomb was found to be empty. At the same time, he was seen alive by a few. Later, he was seen alive by many. He was seen to be living a new life. Go figure.

Spend this day in awe. A thirst for detail will profit you nothing. Easter is for being caught up. Let your feet lift off the ground, stick your head in that cloud. And praise God for what you know must be true.

Someone else can explain how cold flesh grew warm again, how a heart drained of life began to beat, how arteries and veins well past their final constriction opened to receive the rush of new purpose. But not you, not today. Today is

Easter Sunday

for Alleluias, for promises kept and promises given. He has risen as he said he would. He has risen to be the first-born of many brothers and sisters.

> morning mists bedew the brain
> enraptured by the ant-
> ic   i c something
> guileless gawkers crane their necks
> to peer around the log-
> ic   i c someone
> yearning hearts reverberate
> in time with heaven's mus-
> ic   i c movement
> whirling souls resist the grip
> of arguments pedant-
> ic   i c new life
> brittle reason falls to dust
> as pundits turn to pan -
> ic   i c my hope
> death by love is overcome
> prosaic by iamb -
> ic   i c the Son

Risen Lord, let me drift upon the river of life this day. Protect me from duty, routine, and calculation. Refresh me with the spirit of Easter, the spirit of serene and confident hope.   Amen.

MONDAY OF THE OCTAVE OF EASTER

> My heart has been glad and my tongue has
> rejoiced,
> my body will live on in hope,
> for you will not abandon my soul to
> the nether world,
> nor will you suffer your faithful
> one to undergo corruption.
> You have shown me the paths of life;
> you will fill me with joy in your
> presence   (Acts 2:26-28).

True joy must be rooted in reality. It is impossible to accept the gift of the Resurrection without adverting to the opposite eventuality.

Cynthia appears to be a well-balanced young grandmother. She bore three children early in her marriage. They followed her example, each marrying before the age of twenty. Her only boy became a father last year. Her husband, in his mid-forties, is steady, has a secure job at the plant, and is devoted to her. Cynthia says her prayers at night, goes to Mass each Sunday, and keeps the Holy Days. She plays bridge on Tuesday, makes most of her own clothes, and works about ten hours each week at a coupon redemption center. She can't remember the last time she was really happy and suspects that profound joy is something she will never experience in this life. Nevertheless, she blows the dust off her Bible, determined to give it one more try.

There are many Cynthias among us, good people deprived of inner happiness because they have never seriously examined their own mortality. St. Peter might as well be speaking Chinese when he quotes the 16th Psalm. What can he mean by a glad heart? What does a tongue sound like when it rejoices? Cynthia reads the words, acknowledges that Peter is filled with the spirit of promise, but doubts that he speaks to her. He is using the psalm to reassure the followers of Jesus who were devastated by the Master's death, a subject she considered morbid. At the same time, he is trying to persuade the Jews that the Resurrection answers the unanswerable question. They, like Cynthia, are too set in their humdrum ways to pay him much mind.

Are you too secure to heed Peter's words? Our society makes no secret of its flight from the reality of death. Celebrity and consumerism have successfully drawn us away from the contemplation of the unanswerable question. When daily life seems so durable, the gift of eternal life lies unclaimed.

The days of Easter are not meant to produce a placid loss of memory. The scent of corruption, the taste of the nether world which Peter draws forth from the psalm forcefully reminds us of Christ's passion and death. It happened to him, and it will happen to each of us no matter how assiduously we hold our noses and camouflage the abyss. True joy will not come to Cynthia or any of us until we immerse ourselves in Christ's suffering. Death is the villain of the piece. Nothing less than dying with Jesus will allow us to experience the joy of his victory.

Cynthia will do well to read the Bible with both hands during the next fifty days. The exhilarating proclamation of a glorious rebirth must be rooted in the bloody truth of the Way of the Cross. Join Cynthia today. Balance your meditation on the path to new life with a sober acceptance of mortality.

He came back slowly from the night,
escaped the grip of force obscure;
the hand upon his heart so tight
relaxed with breath's new-found allure.
No time to ask how close the call
or who had taken off his tie;
enough to see the busy mall
and smile at gawking passers-by.
The world looked foreign from down here
stretched out upon the cool cement.
The harried faces bending near
to see a medical event
seemed disappointed when they learned
the snare was slipped before their eyes.
He stood; they hurriedly returned
to Shopping Land where no one dies.
You'll see him there one busy day
come back to muse on his rebirth.
A wiser man, above the fray,
he learned from death what life is worth.

God of the living, grant me a more profound appreciation of the gift of life so that I may accept the treasure of the Resurrection with gratitude and joy. Amen.

TUESDAY OF THE OCTAVE OF EASTER

Jesus said to her, "Mary!" She turned to him and said [in Hebrew], "Rabbouni!" [meaning "Teacher"]. Jesus then said: "Do not cling to me, for I have not yet ascended to the Father. Rather, go to my brothers and tell them, 'I am ascending to my Father and your Father, to my God and your God.' " Mary Magdalene went to the disciples. "I have seen the Lord," she announced. Then she reported what he had said to her. (John 20:16-18).

In *The Last Temptation of Christ*, Nikos Kazantzakis draws the picture of a Jesus who escaped death on the cross, a putative Savior who, by the grace of God or the tenacity of the life force, awoke not in a tomb but in a Jerusalem hovel. Nursed by a good woman, he regained his health and took her home with him as his wife. He spent the rest of his life in his beloved Galilee, attained a ripe age and the status of a rustic seer. The fecund earth clung to him and he became the father of many children. He did not become the firstborn from the dead.

In pondering the possibility of an outcome at variance with the historical fact of the Resurrection, we take note of the Master's warning to Mary Magdalene not to deter him from the completion of the Paschal Mystery. Until Jesus took his rightful place in heaven, he would be of little help to us. True, we could honor him as a paragon of goodness. Our attempt to imitate his trust in his Father would be quite meritorious in itself. Heartfelt prayers to be accorded the same favor he received on Easter morning would certainly please God. But to want to cling only to the memory of a selfless rabbi as Mary did, or even to clutch at the knees of a man simply returned from the dead, would be to love this life too much. Kazantzakis shows us that a good man is indeed hard to find. In his story, the memory of the carpenter's son lived for a while in the collective psyche of the people of Nazareth. When enough Galileans died, so did the memory.

Jesus had to be more than a pleasant memory. He had to be the Christ, and not merely the anointed liberator of a hapless nation, but the eternally living Son of God. Not just the resurrected one, or even the firstborn of many brothers and sisters, he had to be the divinely empowered Savior, the Omega Man, the path to ultimate union with God. The man from Nazareth was bound to carry through his mission, to be at the same time our Guide and our Goal.

He was all this, and all this by choice. In that mysterious human-divine dynamic which defined his essence, Jesus decided to complete his work. He was what he chose to be under no compulsion but love. His denial of the Magdalene's implicit invitation to cling to her was but one more manifestation of his self-emptying choice in favor of a chance for you and me, another witness to his preference to save despite the always present danger that he himself would be lost.

Pause today to think of how it might have been. The last temptation of Christ was like all the other inducements, both darkly satanic and warmly human, to hold on to the world for dear life. Because he held the life of his brothers and sisters so dear, he chose to let go of life. The rescue in which we rejoice this week is all the more gratifying precisely because it was not obligatory. It was a matter of choice.

>Mounting to the stars
>he saw the throne of God
>ablaze against an ebon sky.
>
>Pausing in mid-stride
>he turned his gaze upon
>the riven earth's sad supplicants.
>
>Bending to their prayers
>he brushed the clinging clay
>from winged heel and made his mark.
>
>Leaping toward the dawn
>he left a footprint clear
>enough to guide a yearning world.

Jesus Lord, through you all humankind was made in the image and likeness of the Father. Through our folly we continually distort the reflection of his love. Straighten our ways. Lead us back to our source and our salvation. Amen.

WEDNESDAY OF THE OCTAVE OF EASTER

> Then Jesus said to them, "What little sense you have! How slow you are to believe all that the prophets have announced! Did not the Messiah have to undergo all this so as to enter into his glory?" Beginning, then, with Moses and all the prophets, he interpreted for them every passage of Scripture which referred to him. By now they were near the village to which they were going, and he acted as if he were going farther. But they pressed him: "Stay with us. It is nearly evening—the day is practically over." So he went in to stay with them (Luke 24:25-26).

Twilight on the first day of the New Creation. Huddled in a room in Jerusalem, ten men listen for the clatter in the street which will announce their demise. Expecting to hear at any moment the metallic ring of a centurion's light armor, they argue the wisdom of remaining in this city of death when so many of their brothers have fled. Perhaps undercover of the advancing darkness they might . . . but no, the word from the still sobbing Peter was to wait until he returned from calming those hysterical women at the sepulcher. What had they said? Something about the stone. . . ?

Seven miles away, two lesser lights grow dim in the darkness as they make for little Emmaus, their first haven in a desperate flight from calamity. It had all collapsed so quickly, just a few days from Hosannas to that strangled cry on the cross. Their ears are still smarting from the jeers and the thunder as the quiet voice of a stranger pierces their inner turmoil. His words have the caressing appeal of a gentle breeze, a subtle power which calls to flame the dying embers of hope in their hearts.

In the city, Peter climbs the shadowed stairs. He and his brothers, fearful of lighting a telltale candle, begin to exchange confusing whispers about an empty tomb just as a spark of recognition is warming two bleak hearts on the northwest road. The stranger tells the whole story; rather than glossing over the ugly events of the last three days, he explains how each step on the road to Calvary fulfilled a requirement of the ancient prophecies. Anxious escape slows with the realization that it all had to come to pass if the glory were to shine through. The radiance of faith rekindled begins to push back the darkness of fear. The enveloping shadows are checked as wonder and gratitude glisten in widening eyes. "Stay with us." Hold back the night.

Two men too much alone, despairing of their dreams, meet a stranger in their flight. To you, too, he comes with consolation, but not as a stranger. You know Jesus as triumphant even as you bend under the weight of your cares. At Emmaus, he revealed himself in the breaking open of the Scriptures and the breaking of the bread. They saw the rightness of his suffering, how necessary it was for him to be lost so that they might be saved. Even in the midst of your travail, you experience the happy serenity of one beloved as you advance to the altar of sacrifice. Now, in holy communion with the Suffering Servant, you return from the banquet of life not in flight but as a living witness to hope reborn. And just as the two starstruck disciples ran back to Jerusalem to add their good news to the Apostles' incredible discoveries, you set out with joy to inform your world of its rebirth.

> the quaking aspen in the gale
> the nervous bride behind her veil
> the smile upon the haggard face
> the hindmost runner in the race
> the crocus poking through the snow
> the bud of yeast within the dough
> the truth beneath a sea of lies
> the songbird in a world of sighs
> the crucifix behind the bier
> the tiny flame within a tear
> is hope

Holy Spirit of life, breathe upon the spark of hope hidden deep within our hearts. Fan it to a flame to light the way for all who walk in twilight. Amen.

THURSDAY OF THE OCTAVE OF EASTER

> While they were still speaking about all this, (Jesus) himself stood in their midst [and said to them, "Peace to you."] In their panic and fright they thought they were seeing a ghost. He said to them, "Why are you disturbed? Why do such ideas cross your mind? Look at my hands and my feet; it is really I. Touch me, and see that a ghost does not have flesh and bones as I do" (Luke 24:36-39).

To say that the Apostles were surprised by the post-Resurrection appearances would be an egregious understatement, but to say that they were unprepared would be a mistake. In ways subtle and not so subtle, Jesus had nurtured their immature faith, teaching them that after three days "this temple" would be raised up. True, honest men could disagree about whether he spoke of a building in Jerusalem or his own body, but could there be any dispute over the bald declaration that the Gentiles would carry out the designs of the chief priests and scribes by killing him, "but three days later he will rise" (Mark 10:34)?

The answer from the Upper Room is obvious. Panic and fright are hardly the emotions prompted by the anticipated fulfillment of a cherished prophecy. Despite Jesus' earnest persuasion, his closest followers were not ready to believe in the Good News. Even as they probed his risen flesh with tentative fingers, even as joy filled their hearts as they watched him eat a piece of fish, the Master's students flunked the test of faith. "They were still incredulous for sheer joy and wonder" (John 24:41). From panic and fright to joy and wonder, faith was the tortoise, emotion the hare.

This is a good day to take the temperature of your approach to religion. So many seek the spectacular, the hot medium, the preacher convicting the cowed congregants of the most heinous sins, the throbbing rhythms manipulating metanoia, the demanding healer vindicated by the swooning invalid. Religion in the glare of the spotlight is always suspect. The public eye is fickle and unfocussed; it tires even of the fantastic and in its restlessness overlooks the detail, the essential, the truth.

To let emotion rule your worship is to abandon the search for a reasonable God. Sensations which outrace faith cannot take one anywhere; they are of the moment with no future or past. Jesus, fresh-risen from the grave, would not immediately sweep his awestruck friends into a new dimension precisely because the weight of their feelings anchored them to the present moment. It is a misnomer to say that one is "transported" by joy or wonder; a person overcome by emotion is pressed into the now.

Faith is forward-looking. The believer sees the future as reasonable. God's universe is intelligible, at least to God; we are permitted to understand a part of God's plan because of our intelligence, not our emotions. It would take the Apostles the rest of their lives to decode the Paschal event, and then only with a massive dose of wisdom thanks to the Holy Spirit. Jesus ate a piece of fish to calm the emotions of the moment so that reason's light could begin to illuminate tomorrow's ministry.

In this week of glory, we give ourselves to joy, to a moment of high triumph, to the savoring of a lived instant of rapture. Yet we are wise enough to know that, when feeling fades, faith remains. Tomorrow, we may not be in seventh heaven, but we will still believe.

> In water swiftly flowing, solemn Heraclitus spied
> the face Demeter turned to men who long for joys divine.
> A rush of passion rudely thrust both thought and glance aside,
> and bending low he stretched to kiss a natant porcupine.

Risen Lord, we are swept away by your astounding victory over death. When the radiance fades, help us to meditate quietly on the meaning of Easter in our everyday lives. May faith be our guide on the path to inner peace.   Amen.

FRIDAY OF THE OCTAVE OF EASTER

> This is the day the Lord had made;
> let us be glad and rejoice in it.
> O Lord, grant salvation!
> O Lord, grant prosperity!
> Blessed is he who comes in the name of the Lord;
> we bless you from the house of the Lord
> (Psalm 118:24-26).

The weather forecasters, painfully aware that they had pushed the panic button once too often, did not refer to it as a storm. Just a tropical depression, bumping around in the northern Gulf of Mexico, overlaying the soggy land now here, now there, it was a nuisance to be tolerated, a threat only to the shallowest skiffs. The rain came not in torrents but as delicate veils, silvery curtains descending from a leaden sky. The cumulative effect was powerful, though. The incessant humidity, the palpable weight of the lowering clouds, the implicit burden of a mile-high column of water upon the brain combined to wilt even Pollyanna's curls.

There must be days which God disavows, sodden spools of hours which he has not made, unwinding in crazy knots and tangles from the loom of life to become a fowler's net of care sticking to the skin of the soul, constricting industry and ambition, pinioning the wings of hope. Let us rejoice and be glad, indeed!

In his acceptance speech before the 1949 Nobel Prize Committee, William Faulkner did not assure the world that each dawn was the Lord's doing. He made it plain that more often than not men and women must go it alone, that the only necessary, the only lasting human virtue was quite empty of romance; he knew it as endurance. To his fictional

Friday of the Octave of Easter

Yoknapatawpha County, Mississippi stretched the clammy fingers of many a tropical storm. The rolling moisture diluted the spirit of mutual concern, tarnished the burnished bonds of fellowship. In this corrosive atmosphere, the human animal hunkered down to wait out the sullen sky, to endure the games of fate.

Yoknapatawpha *is* the world, of course, and each of us sojourners there. Yoknapatawpha is Good Friday and February 15, 1898 and August 6, 1945. We are Jews and jingoes and Japanese, and there are some days in which we cannot rejoice, some days which make us doubt whether God's heart is bigger than that of a truant officer. These are the days when we can do no better than to take the advice of a world-weary novelist, and endure.

Paul of Tarsus knew these days as well as William Faulkner. To the Christians of Rome he wrote of the sufferings of the present and the glory to come. His tone was measured, his advice practical. Unlike Faulkner, he was not afraid to speak of a better day, but his own trials had taught him that tomorrow pleads for a thousand dawns. Always sensitive to the groans of a world in agony, he too affirmed the virtue of holding on. The visionary of the Damascus road speaks to us just six days after we've celebrated the fulfillment of humankind's fondest hope. When the lightning flash of the Resurrection blinds us to the pitfalls of the everyday and our stumbled souls lie prone under clouds swollen with cares, life for a while consists in "hoping for what we cannot see" and "awaiting it with patient endurance" (Romans 8:25).

> Behind sepulchral stone a fierce
> and saving beam begins to pierce
> time and rock
> space and death.

>   Then freed to seek the spirits bound
>   it sweeps the universe around
>   warning all
>   souls who were
>   and who will be discouraged by
>   the swelling clouds in Easter's sky.
>   *Slow, bright Sun!*
>   *Here am I.*
>   The rescued hail this comfort pure
>   and light while others must endure
>   dark and damp
>   one more day.

Lord of the everyday, give us courage in our trials, teach us that endurance need not mean acceptance, help us to hold on while we keep on. Whenever our way is shadowed, send Christ, our Light, to lead us. Amen.

SATURDAY OF THE OCTAVE OF EASTER

> Finally, as they were at table, Jesus was revealed to the Eleven. He took them to task for their disbelief and their stubbornness, since they had put no faith in those who had seen him after he had been raised. Then he told them: "Go into the whole world and proclaim the good news to all creation"   (Mark 16:14-15).

chiaroscuro: *key-ahr-uh-skoor'-oh* (Italian) The arrangement of light and dark elements in a pictorial representation.

The Octave of Easter is a frieze in chiaroscuro, a series of scenes in which the light of the Resurrection contends with shadows of disbelief. During this week, we have seen angels in dazzling garments and refugees stumbling in the darkness. Hearts have burned with recognition, hearts have shriveled in fear. The Risen Lord has appeared with words of comfort and peace only to be met with panic. His closest followers doubted and dithered.

Two thousand years later, fastidious Christians still sit on the fence. Unsure whether to laugh or cry, they await a more definitive revelation to purify their intentions.

Men and women of good faith, priests filled with a yearning for renewal, parents well aware of the example their children need to see, business people apprehensive over what passes for ethics in the world of commerce shiver like magnetized compasses at the thought of telling the good news. Just one more indication that Jesus conquered death is all they need, one more proof that the Risen Christ stands in their midst, then they would make bold proclamation.

Like the Eleven lingering in the Upper Room, too many children of the Resurrection hesitate to claim their patrimony, afraid to get too far ahead of the crowd lest the message of the empty tomb prove to be a fantasy of smoke and mirrors. There is something in the soul of modern society that won't take "Yes" for an answer. The result: stagnation in the marketplace of ideas. Or worse, capitulation to the inexorable march of secularism. If important segments of human concourse are off limits to the influence of Christian values, it is because many who ostensibly hold these values remain unconvinced or even fearful of the power of renewal which is the essence of the Good News. These dormant Christians lie low, brooding upon the dark and light of the Paschal Mystery, waiting for further clarification, listening for the Better News.

Christ will not wait. Today's Gospel passage is a sorry list of grieving and weeping, inertia and disbelief, ending not with the Master's understanding consolation but with his rebuke. "Get cracking!" he seems to say. "The world will always be in chiaroscuro. The radiance of my rising pushed back the darkness; it didn't eradicate it. Don't wait for the perfect moment. The time is now. There would be no need for the Good News if bad news didn't persist. Go into the world that is, the land of twilight, and light a fire in the shadows."

Take a moment to picture the sunless reaches in your life and in the lives of those around you. Then recall the radiance of the Resurrection. It is precisely that contrast which is our motive and our joy.

> The night comes solid up against the cross
> then warily delays as Rembrandt kindles tiny twigs
> a torch to limn.
> Soon pallid flesh returns the golden glow
> yet quickens not nor would if Holland's sun looked down
> upon Jerusalem.
> Old Nicodemus bends beneath the weight
> and weeps with her who carried once a fragile flame of hope
> to Bethlehem.
> Now blind with sorrow, they shall see that Light
> from Light descended, struck a spark of life against the void,
> and will again.

Father of light, in the reflected glory of the Resurrection, we stand with arms upraised to praise your name. Into our darkness, you have plunged the fire of your divine love, a love which has taken our flesh and illuminated our way. We thank you for each tiny spark of life and for the bright Sun of life renewed.   Amen.

SECOND SUNDAY OF EASTER

A week later, the disciples were once more in the room, and this time Thomas was with them. Despite the locked doors, Jesus came and stood before them. "Peace be with you," he said; then, to Thomas: "Take your finger and examine my hands. Put your hand into my side. Do not persist in your unbelief, but believe!" Thomas said in response, "My Lord and my God!" Jesus then said to him:
> "You became a believer because
>   you saw me.
> Blest are they who have not seen
>   and have believed"   (John 20:26-29)

During sister's visits, old Mr. Fanucci sat bolt upright in bed, his arms folded defiantly across his chest. To master his arthritic body even for fifteen minutes was always a source of pride, a feat much more difficult than his curt and consistent refusal of the sacrament. Indeed, rejection of the body of the Christ who would not rescue him gave rise to a perverse pleasure. Nothing, however, could match his sense of accomplishment each First Friday when he was privileged to order the timid Father Angelo out of his room.

As the ancient nun caressed her message of submission, he pushed away the pain with a private litany of betrayal: the initial anger at the curvature of his limbs and spine; his many hospitalizations during the fifth of which his wife had died; his arrival at the Home three years ago; the subsequent abandonment by his children. He tasted the bitterness of being "old Mr. Fanucci" at fifty-seven. Sister creaked when she stood up, then made a half-hearted gesture toward the pyx hanging from her neck. He waved her away vigorously, proud of the line of his arm, proud of the strength of his disbelief. Once more, he had passed the test which he allowed only her to administer; he had seen nothing that wasn't there.

Relieved of her cloying concern, he let his body recoil to become again the "elbow macaroni" with which he reproached his children during their infrequent telephone calls. ("To you, I'm pasta," he would growl, effectively ending the conversation.) The pain subsided to that of a bed of nails; he dozed on sharp points of resentment.

Something drew him back, something was missing. The dog that didn't bark. The door that didn't slam. That rickety sister had left the castle gate ajar again. With effort he opened his eyes and saw that the door was quite secure, in fact, wedged shut as Sister Mary Philip Zito, C.F.M. slumped against it in her slow descent to the floor.

As he fumbled for the call button, her head hung for a long moment on the doorknob, then dropped heavily to the terrazzo. The crack of bone on stone reminded him that his hardheadedness frequently provoked the nurses to ignore his light. So be it. Let it be on their heads.

So quiet. Her strangled breathing accentuated the hush of halls in siesta. The orderlies were probably in their soundproof lounge making fun of the residents and smoking pot. He moaned against the slow uncoiling of his body, against the labored resurrection of his conscience. He concentrated on what would be required of his limbs when they touched the floor, tried to recall the demands of balance and locomotion. In the end, he fell from the bed and shared with her the sharp kiss of terrazzo. Then, hand and knee, he crawled to the still decorous folds of the black habit.

Could he touch a nun, a virgin consecrated to God? What was that to him anymore? He turned her head toward the window and placed it in her forearm. "Oh, Father Angelo," she murmured, "I'm going home." He sat back on his protesting haunches. "I'm not Father Angelo!" he roared. She spoke rapidly now, "Hear my confession, Father." "I'm Fanucci. Tom Fanucci! You were visiting me." In a breathless singsong she began with the time since her last Confession, offered the short list of a pious woman in vows, then waited for Absolution.

He waited too. For the first time in years, he waited for rescue. He waited for her salvation, and for his. He waited for a Word.

"*Ad Deum qui laetificat . . .*" It was the voice of a boy in a black cassock kneeling beside a mumbling Monsignor. By the time he finished the Prayers at the Foot of the Altar, someone was pushing open the door against her body. She was carried into the hall, he to his bed. He solidly refused sedation, preferring to remain alert to the flood of memories streaming from his childhood in the Church. It had been so good then, so secure, so alive with faith. After supper, pale Father Angelo looked in to be surprised by a smile. "I just wanted you to know that Sister's doing fine." "Thank God," he said, and then, "Father, can you stop by tomorrow, please? Anytime, at your convenience. Tonight, I'm a bit preoccupied." As always, he spent a long while adjusting each muscle to find an endurable balance of pain. But instead of the customary curses, he said very slowly one Our Father, one Hail Mary, and one Glory Be, once . . . Sister Mary Philip's penance.

Eight days from Easter. Objectivity can no longer be held at bay. With cold logic comes the admission that you and I lack the patience to believe without seeing. The grimace, the scowl, the angry words are enough to send us elsewhere; we will not make the effort to look beyond the forbidding features of an old man Fanucci as Sister Mary Philip did every Tuesday afternoon. Behind those bitter eyes, she saw a man in need. She answered the lonely cry he denied in himself and unwittingly prepared him to answer hers the day she fell against the door. Need spoke to need. Blest was he who saw her want and answered it. Yet, more blessed was she who saw beyond his doubt, and believed.

>   traffic snarling at the line
> crosswalk
>   white cane
>   proffered arm
> need and rescue intertwine
> who keeps
>   whom from
>   sudden harm

Saving Lord, to trust your unseen power is not always easy in a world which puts appearances first. Draw me to the truth within as I join the Gospel supplicant and cry: I believe; help my unbelief. Amen.

MONDAY OF THE SECOND WEEK

A certain Pharisee named Nicodemus, a member of the Jewish Sanhedrin, came to Jesus at night. "Rabbi," he said, "we know you are a teacher come from God, for no man can perform signs and wonders such as you perform unless God is with him." Jesus gave him this answer:
"I solemnly assure you,
no one can see the reign of God
unless he is begotten from above."
"How can a man be born again once he is old?" retorted Nicodemus. "Can he return to his mother's womb and be born all over again?"   (John 3:1-4).

Taking up the lamp of life renewed, we let its revealing beam play over the significant events which led up to the Resurrection. The Gospel of John guides us to a meeting in Jerusalem between a quintessential Jew and a wonder-worker lately notorious for an incident at the Temple. Nicodemus — a member of the Sanhedrin, a Pharisee, and a rabbi — sidles out of the night with ambivalent feelings about this Jesus from Nazareth whom he recognizes as "a teacher come from God." As a member of the highest councils, he is understandably concerned about a country preacher who interrupted the smooth flow of commerce in the Temple. At the same time, he is attracted to the man's self-sufficiency, the air of personal authority which permeates his teaching. Beyond this, however, are the signs and wonders; Jesus would not be the object of this furtive visit had his reputation for the miraculous not preceded him. Finally, there is the challenge: words in accents Galilean which brook no vacillation.

Nicodemus' dilemma is as modern as today. Many of us are of two minds about Jesus. We are drawn to the seamless garment of his truth. His teaching provides an integrated construct for living which consoles and sustains us. Many of us have prayed for miracles of healing and inner peace and have seen our prayers answered. Yet we shrink from the total cost of following the way of Christ, from the demands of altruism which chafe our habitual egocentricity. To invite Jesus into our hearts means that we must allow him at times to wield his whip of cords and cleanse our lives of selfishness and pride. So, we play Nicodemus' game of circumspection and stealth. It is not practical to be too open about our association with this firebrand; he may ask more than we are willing to pay. Retreat is easier in the darkness.

In such a frame of mind, with Nicodemus we welcome the radical statement. When Jesus says that "no one can see the reign of God unless he is begotten from above," we favor the most extreme reading. "How can a man be born again . . . ?" This is our insurance policy. This kind of teaching is what we pull out of our back pocket when Jesus calls upon those who would follow him to go forth into a hostile world without sandals or staff. Just as no one can "return to his mother's womb," so no one is expected to give up all attachments to the world in order to rely completely on Providence. Thus, since the original declaration was flawed by exaggeration, all subsequent commissions must be "modified" to fit the dimensions of the real world.

In the following days, we shall be made to admit what we already know, that Jesus was telling Nicodemus of a new birth from above, a discipleship sprung from water and the Spirit. For now, it is enough to examine our ambivalent approach to his truth. To come to Christ protected by a plan of retreat, to seek him under cover of darkness is to make ourselves the practical masters of the encounter. Backing into discipleship may insure a quick and inconspicuous escape, but it is hardly the stance of sincerity.

> A word to the wise with gentle inflection,
> a friendly nudge in the right direction:
> Invite me, Lord, to mend my ways
> but tolerate a few delays.
>
> Don't startle me with your bold proclamation
> or let my slouch cause you consternation.
> I'll amble home at my own pace
> assured of your amazing grace.
>
> What if, from the throne, his ultimate question
> demands a Yes, not a bland suggestion
> or fickle pledge, but here and now
> commitment when I don't know how?

Master Teacher, let the power of your truth shatter the pride of self which reigns over our lives. Make our hearts supple, pliant, fecund, so that the seed of your word may produce good fruit: faith in your testimony, conformity to your will. Amen.

TUESDAY OF THE SECOND WEEK

> Jesus said to Nicodemus:
> "I solemnly assure you,
> do not be surprised that I tell you
> you must all be begotten from above.
> The wind blows where it will.
> You hear the sound it makes
> but you do not know where it comes from,
>   or where it goes.
> So it is with everyone begotten of
>   the Spirit"   (John 3:7-8).

The canyons of the city swirl with diving birds and fluttering scraps of paper. Planners and profitmakers thrust into the blameless sky towers of glass and stone; in turn, affronted nature fashions her answer, sending it forth to seek out nook and aperture, to chafe the shimmering spires, a measured reply, steady, eternal: the wind.

A gray man at a gray desk looks down upon the whirling wings and knows precisely where the wind comes from; it comes from the north to madden sparrow and starling, secretary and assistant auditor. And he knows where it goes: nosing into the echoing chambers that frame hearts barely beating, hearts that were once alive with curiosity and promise. A gray man suddenly realizes that his heart has cooled with the years; what he thought was adequate warmth is overwhelmed by this chilling rebuke from the heavens. Reflected in the window are green figures from the computer screen, a thousand bits of memory frozen in space.

The soaring office tower contends with the power of truth. Sculptured granite and leaded glass amplify the insistent voice. A gray man learns the history of his heart's capitulation, the glacial passage from youthful optimism to mid-life resignation. Unnoticed until now, the pure flame that once would burn away the corruption of this world has become a fitfully glowing ember. And would remain so, if not for this urgent northern breath which at the same time proves the impotence of hope grown dim and rudely calls forth a feeble flame. There in a swaying skyscraper, the spirit of God will kill or cure; there in a quaking breast, a heart becomes a crucible.

It is indeed a chill wind that fans no flame. The Spirit of God called forth courage from the fearful hearts of Isaiah and Jeremiah; it is the same spirit which will hover in the Upper Room and make of stooped spines pure steel. The barriers which we throw up against this questing spirit are like the great buildings in our cities, constructed for comfort, airtight to protect us from the harsh elements. In the routine of ritualism and arm's-length charity, we spend our days husbanding a tiny flame of faith. Yet, our greatest fear is not that the mighty breath of God will blow it out; more daunting is our suspicion that his spirit will call forth the fire of idealism and we will get burned as we have so often in the past.

Today, let the wind blow where it will. The sound it makes is a call for renewal. If it shakes your defenses, know that the Spirit has taken hold of you. If it fans to new flame the spark of reform, let yourself be consumed. Do not fear even if the shock of truth turns sputtering embers to lifeless cinders. Once, on a dark Friday afternoon, the fire went out of the whole world, only to be born again in the hearts of eleven men as cold as you and I.

> green wood oozing
> > lifeblood as a new fire
> > snaps and
> > sizzles
>
> searching for a better hold
> > on green wood
>
> consumed are nights of love and sunshot days
> reduced are wordless vows and frank displays
> foredoomed are brazen glance and tender gaze
>
> dry wood yielding
> > falling into old fire
> > sighs and
> > whispers
>
> when the hearth of life depends
> > on dry wood

Lord Jesus, no day is dull, no task routine when we recognize your presence in the little things of life. Make us sensitive to your call in the ticking of a clock, to your love in the humdrum. Help us to see each dawn as the opening of a treasure-trove of opportunities for growth in your grace.   Amen.

WEDNESDAY OF THE SECOND WEEK

> Jesus said to Nicodemus:
> > "God did not send the Son into the world
> > to condemn the world,

> but that the world might be saved through him.
> Whoever believes in him avoids condemnation,
> but whoever does not believe
>   is already condemned
> for not believing in the name
>   of God's only Son" (John 3:17-18).

An involuntary shudder is a natural reaction to the subject of God's final judgment. Even the most righteous among us loses a bit of self-assurance when contemplating a picture of the Son of Man separating the sheep from the goats and pointing the latter toward the bubbling brimstone. Many in our society attempt to counter fear of ultimate damnation by denying the existence of hell. A recent survey of the general population without regard to religious affiliation found that only 37% of Americans believed that there is a place or state of eternal punishment. No doubt many of those in the majority would say that a loving God could not be that mean; he must give everyone a last chance at repentance. Perhaps he does. Given his Son's record of forgiveness, it wouldn't be surprising to find that God offers an opportunity for a change of heart at the heart's last beating. But that doesn't preclude the necessity of the abyss. Some hearts will not change; even God will be powerless in the face of ingrained contrariness.

In today's passage from the Gospel according to John, Jesus describes himself as a judge, not in the sense of one who renders a condemnatory verdict, but rather as a model of right living for humankind. How far we deliberately diverge from that model in the area of moral choice is the measure of our sinfulness, our self-condemnation. A lifetime of grievous deviation from the Way, the Truth, and the Life does not bode well for a deathbed conversion. Even if there is a last chance, habits die hard.

Those who say that God has never condemned anyone to hell may be correct, but they are sadly mistaken in their conclusion that hell doesn't exist. There must be a separate state of being after death for those who spend their lives hating God and contravening his laws. If heaven held a place for the lifelong philanderer *and* his constant wife, could God's word ever be credible? If the unrepentant child molester *and* his innocent prey will be in the same number, could Jesus' stern warnings have any validity? If the genocidal tyrants of recent history share even a moment of their victims' eternal reward, could the urgings of the Holy Spirit be trusted? Would it not be a cosmic joke on his creatures, the ultimate April Fool trick, if God were to conjoin for eternity those who sacrificed and suffered to uphold the principles his Son taught and those who mocked those teachings with every choice they made?

God does not play tricks on his struggling people, nor is he an Indian giver. In empowering us to choose freely, he made it possible for us to turn away from his love. We began at once to do just that, but still he would not take back the gift of free will. Instead, he sent his Son to urge us to choose life; if we choose death, he will honor our decision. Jesus taught us a way of living, and more, he lived it. If we turn our backs on his sublime example and practice a way of dying, God will not force us into heaven.

Spend a solemn, heart-wrenching moment of regret over your own acts of self-condemnation. Each was a step in the wrong direction, a movement away from God and his house of many dwelling places. Each time a moral decision was at variance with the choice Jesus would have made, you inched closer to proving that 63% of Americans are dead wrong about hell. Not a happy reverie, by any means, but necessary from time to time for those who would rather leave the proof to someone else.

> The endless night reverberates
> with melancholy cries
> of those who see the face of God
> but once when daylight dies.
> This final fleeting glimpse of love
> will weigh on desperate eyes
> forever to remind the lost
> of where their treasure lies.

Saving Lord, save us from the folly of not fearing hell. We readily admit that our stubbornness and pride can overpower nicely-reasoned arguments and delicate principles which encourage right living. When we turn our backs on your gentle invitation, make us face the abyss just long enough to shock us back to sanctity. Amen.

THURSDAY OF THE SECOND WEEK

> Jesus said to Nicodemus:
> "The One who comes from heaven
>   [who is above all]
> testifies to what he has seen and heard,
> but no one accepts his testimony.
> Whoever does accept this testimony
> certifies that God is truthful.
> For the One whom God has sent
> speaks the words of God;
> he does not ration his gifts of the Spirit.
> The Father loves the Son
> and has given everything over to him"
>   (John 3:31-35).

In the comic strip, "Li'l Abner," the folks who made Dogpatch come alive for millions of readers were caricatures of the best and worst in each of us. Daisy Mae's stunningly-endowed lassitude, Mammy's outspoken common sense, Abner's stalwart naivete were what Al Capp saw in the American psyche. Of all the good and bad apples on the Yokum family tree, no one was more respected than cousin "C. C." When the threat of some dire calamity demanded nerves of steel, he got the call. "C. C." Yokum could ignore the most voluptuous of the holler's easy women, pass right by a platter heaped high with grits and jowls, and then amble through the cemetery on Halloween with an unhurried step. "C. C." — the initials always appeared in quotation marks to highlight the awe he commanded from the mountain people — stood for Complete Control.

In the life of a Christian, the steely insensibility of "C. C." Yokum points to that restraining impulse which limits the ability to receive and to give the gift of the Spirit. Today's passage from the Gospel of John teaches that the giver of the gift sets no limits; "he does not ration" the revelation of his love for humankind. Into Jesus Christ, he poured his complete concern for the world, a commitment so perfect as to become a person, and not just any person, but the living Son and Savior. Jesus is the perfect personification of the Father's passionate attraction to you and me; he is love incarnate, love radiating love.

The "C. C." Yokum in us says, "Watch out!" This radiant gift may be a Trojan Horse, a way of outflanking our defenses in order to subvert from within our self-control. Once we let the Spirit of God act within us, it will overwhelm our plans for our own perfection. Take care not to fall into the arms of God; his love will melt your hardened hearts and you will become no more than sheep led to the slaughter of your autonomy. Beware of God bearing gifts. Maintain Complete Control.

The tragedy of "C. C." Yokum could be seen in his face and carriage. His perpetual frown, severe black suit, and dour demeanor were those of a one-dimensional man, a virtual outcast summoned only in the most dire emergencies, a presence tolerated just until the danger passed. When you and I close ourselves to the searching Spirit of God, when for safety's sake we stand well away from the resplendent love which is Christ, we assume the flat aspect of a cartoon character. There is little to love in us for we allow ourselves to love so little.

Are too many of us completely controlled Christians, giving but faint testimony to the victory of love celebrated in this Resurrection season? If so, that bit of the Good News for which we are responsible is not being heard. We live in a society where thousands openly admit their search for some kind of love. When their honest quest touches our lives, what will we tell them? "I'm all right, Jack. Lots of luck"? Or will we admit that we are searchers too, that we are open to the gift of God's Spirit, that we will accept and bestow without rationing the love which the Father has revealed to us in his Son? The latter course is the more perilous, to be sure, for to be open to love means to be vulnerable to its opposite. We can only proceed by faith, trusting that the gift which God poured out upon the earth in such abundance, the living Love which became our salvation, can overcome any misfortune. Can you think of a greater misfortune than that which took place on Good Friday afternoon? God's love was enough then; it is enough now.

Take time to explore new ways in which his love can shine through you.

Now-talk Christians clipped and cool
those who will not play the fool
murmur of the madding crowd
careful not to speak aloud
lest awakened some dark song
tempt their crystal souls to wrong.

Laid-back mellow buzzwords fly
mask the urge to verify
whispers tickling jaded ears
threatening protective fears
with the news that God just might
tempt us each to do the right.

Lord Jesus, you are the rightful heir of the Father's infinite love, a love which took flesh at your conception, was born into the world, betrayed, raised up, and returned to glory. Make me a more willing beneficiary of that love and help me to follow more closely your example of sharing it. Amen.

FRIDAY OF THE SECOND WEEK

When the people saw the sign he had performed they began to say, "This is undoubtedly the Prophet who is to come into the world." At that, Jesus realized that they would come and carry him off to make him king, so he fled back to the mountain alone   (John 6:14-15).

"Don Bloch finally saw the light. We got his letter yesterday . . . *Uno momento*, dear. Patty's buzzing me."

Her mind raced. She had been working sixteen years for this call. The telephone cord coiled around the rungs on the corporate ladder: Her start in the purchasing department; the long, apparently dead-end years in product development; eons of night classes; the M. B. A.; the rapid promotions in the minority-sensitive Eighties. Yet she was relieved when Masterman's secretary came on to apologize for the long hold. The Director of Personnel had just received an overseas call. Could she wait at her desk for about ten minutes? She put down the receiver as if it were a loaded pistol.

Sixteen years of striving. No, she thought, that was too nice a word for it. Sixteen years of conniving was more like it. She had paid her dues, working harder for the company than anyone she knew. And she had worked hard for herself, flattering her superiors, alerting them to the foibles of her peers. Wisely, she had married out of her department but upscale in the organization. Wisely, she had divorced just before Arnie's drinking became a front office scandal. The split had freed her from the constraint of unspoken policy: No woman rises higher than her husband. In the three years since his transfer, she had hopscotched well beyond Arnie's sinecure, gaining experience and contacts in a dozen operations all over the country. Now the Assistant to the Manager of the Western Region stared at her phone and thought of the empty office down the hall.

It hadn't been difficult to make Donald Bloch look bad. Chicago had always been eager to hear her descriptions of his chronic indecisiveness and bouts of depression; they received her back-channel reviews of his version of Hamlet with gratitude. When western sales slumped noticeably during the last Christmas season, she consoled him, urged him to take some time off at a private burn-out center for executive types. He could tell Chicago he was going to the Bahamas. When he had not returned in two weeks, Masterman knew whom to call for the inside story.

Now there was a month of dust on Don's desk.

Masterman's original query had been the first of many from offices across the country. They all ended the same way: If Bloch would only resign, she had it in the bag. The chrome buttons and pearlescent receiver begged to be touched; no matter which way she repositioned the telephone, it seemed to be pointing at her.

Jesus wouldn't do well in corporate America. If they came to make him department head or plant manager, he would flee "back to the mountain alone." Jesus knew he was beloved by God. When you and I make the approval of our superiors the criterion of self-worth, we are admitting that we don't believe in God's love. When we measure our value according to the loftiness of our position, we are confessing to despair. Confidence in God's loving mercy is foreign to the world of power plays and career wars. The hopelessness of oneupmanship can be seen on any level of human interaction from the boardroom to the Holy Name Society; as soon as men and women lose sight of their ultimate goal, the urge to prove themselves against one another becomes compelling. It is no surprise that so many best-selling books champion aggressiveness and promote strategies for becoming Number One.

Today's Gospel passage offers a simple test for trust in God. When they come bearing scepter and crown, will you be able to flee to the mountain alone?

> Good John, why not a holy book
> that ends with chapter six
> and part of verse fifteen to spare
> us that unseemly mix
> of rank oneupmanship among
> these Galilean hicks?

This amputated Testament
would artfully explain
how from the new Jerusalem
the Nazarene did reign
with twelve content and humble dukes
who never thought of gain.

Of course, to keen librarians
a story minus pride
cries out in such a world as ours
to be reclassified
from Fact to Fantasy and there
with fairy tales abide.

Lord God, we long to be content in the confirmation of your love for us. Open our eyes to the sacrifice of Jesus on the cross, the ultimate proof of our value to you. Let the radiance of the Resurrection enlighten our hearts.   Amen.

SATURDAY OF THE SECOND WEEK

The Twelve assembled the community of the disciples and said, "It is not right for us to neglect the word of God in order to wait on tables. Look around among your own number, brothers, for seven men acknowledged to be deeply spiritual and prudent, and we shall appoint them to this task. This will permit us to concentrate on prayer and the ministry of the word"   (Acts 6:2-4).

The Spirit led the Twelve away sixty stadia from Jerusalem to a high mountain and bade them climb up. At the top they found a valley shrouded in mist. In the center of the valley stood a terebinth upon which lightning played. Inspired to recline around the tree, they fasted there for seven days and seven nights. Early on the morning of the eighth day, the valley floor began to tremble as from an earthquake, and these words appeared to be forged of electrum on the face of a sheer cliff:

> FROM SEVEN MEN SHALL YE NOW ASK
> ASSISTANCE IN EACH MUNDANE TASK.

That's not how it happened at all. No trek to a mountain, no lightning or electrum, rather, complaints about simple community needs moved the Apostles to impose hands on the first deacons of the Church. God works his wonders in the chinks in our lives, in those pencil-thin, painful cracks between the comfortable, solid structures of certainty. There, like a voice in the wilderness, the Spirit calls for healing.

We have heard this insistent voice many times in our land. Twenty-five years ago a call went out for the balm of tolerance and understanding to be poured upon those who perpetuated racial inequality. A distinctive minority, caught between monolithic power and centuries of social habit awakened us to their plight and made us see that segregation was our plight as well. The Spirit spoke not from the mountaintop but from the ghettos and fields; the Spirit spoke not in magistral tones but in accents black. We were made to listen because the voice was the spirit of justice, the spirit of human worth, the Spirit of God, and it was in our midst. Some die-hards still wait to hear the message in the thunder, to see it writ in stone, but they are blind and deaf to simple needs and routine wrongs. Thank God their like were not among the Twelve who listened for the Spirit in the everyday.

To be sensitive to the Spirit is not to search the skies for shooting stars. Such an esoteric occupation invites a certain spiritual elitism, a studied aloofness to the urgings of the Spirit in the rough and tumble of daily life. If, upon being made aware of the need for more hands to portion out the young community's food, the Apostles had gone on retreat sixty stadia from Jerusalem, their flock would have grown only thinner while the proclamation of the Good News languished. Enough of these flights from reality and even their divine mandate could not have made the Twelve credible shepherds.

As committed Christians, we will seek the Master's Spirit in the here and now. He knew that, had he remained on earth, we would be forever sitting at his feet. Wisely taking his leave, he gave the gift of himself to each of those in need so he could weep with them, want with them, cry out in them. That gift, that Spirit waits in the fissures of life, in our broken brothers and sisters. "Why do you stand here looking up at the skies?" he says. Put your ear to the ground and hear my voice.

> Up from their bowels rose the cry.
> Throats aflame, blaspheming over bread,
> mourning Egypt's flesh, they clamored.
> Sweet manna was his gift.
>
> Down from the mountain Moses came,
> face afire, beard streaming in the wind,
> bearing tablets scribed by lightning.
> They danced around the calf.

Patient Father, hear the voice of our wounded world. Though we are often heedless of your saving plan, in times of trouble we are quick to seek your protection. Have mercy on your fickle people. Amen.

THIRD SUNDAY OF EASTER

> When they had eaten their meal, Jesus
> said to Simon Peter, "Simon, son of
> John, do you love me more than these?"
> "Yes, Lord," he said, "you know that
> I love you." At which Jesus said,
> "Feed my lambs."
>
> A second time he put his question,
> "Simon, son of John, do you love me?"
> "Yes, Lord," Peter said, "you know
> that I love you." Jesus replied,
> "Tend my sheep."
>
> A third time Jesus asked him, "Simon,
> son of John, do you love me?"
> Peter was hurt because he had asked
> a third time, "Do you love me?"
> So he said to him: "Lord, you know everything.
> You know well that I love you."
> Jesus said to him,
> "Feed my sheep"   (John 21:15-17).

The lamp of life renewed shines where it will, scattering shades of doubt, illuminating the will of God, pushing back shadows to permit the errant pilgrim a view of the straight path. The radiance of the Resurrection flows through many channels, through the voice of Stephen, the Deacon, urging his countrymen to accept the murdered Jesus as their long-awaited Messiah, through the healing touch of the Apostles when first they ventured forth from the Upper Room to find the sick and the lame beseeching them, through the taste of consecrated bread and wine, the nourishment of the young Christian community.

Prior to and essential to the efficacy of any of these channels of new life is the font of the Father's abundant love, the heart of the Risen Christ. During the process of Resurrection-Ascension-Pentecost, no matter how brief that passage may have been, certain of Jesus' followers were privileged to draw near to that "burning furnace of charity." The Apostles, Mary Magdalene, the men on the Emmaus road, and others were bathed in the radiance of Christ's passion for humankind. The light of this blazing beacon of love was held over Simon Peter in today's Gospel; it pierced and soothed, scorched and cauterized, humbled and empowered.

Three times the soul of the big fisherman was seared until finally in the darkest corner of his conscience a truth began to gleam. It was a hard diamond of truth buried like Jesus in the tomb beneath layers of human pride and fear. There, reflected in the light of Christ's love was an admission of imperfect love: "Lord, you know everything." Peter's protestations of loyalty were riddled with the memory of his treachery. Now, in the steady gaze of the Master, pretence turned to ashes: Lord, you know everything. You know that I haven't loved you enough. You know that as often as I pledged my fidelity, I have betrayed yours. The Rock upon which you set your Church crumbled with the first trembling of the earth in which I am so conspicuously anchored.

As the love of Christ melted the porous foundation of Peter's faith, as it drew forth tears to cool his shame, it healed. Accompanying the sting of self-realization was an invitation to wholeness, a call for Peter to reclaim his former status as a loyal disciple and first among equals. But there was a greater challenge: From the shattered rock would be formed a mighty pillar of faith, a steadfast pedestal to hold the lamp kindled at the Resurrection. "Feed my lambs."

Supported by the mended shards of one man's loyalty, the spirit of the Risen Christ would smile upon the wide world. "Tend my sheep." Strength would shine forth from weakness and renew the face of the earth. "Feed my sheep."

Because our shame is stronger than our faith, few of us would join St. Paul in boasting of our weaknesses (See 2 Corinthians 12:9). But in the radiance of the Resurrection we can give thanks that the mercy of God goes far beyond forgiveness. He extends to us the mercy of mission, the balm of important work; he commissions us to bear the lamp of life renewed into the inner darkness of hearts without hope. Simon Peter became no less impetuous, no more articulate because of the challenge of the Risen Christ. He did, however, become a more apt and willing channel for the Holy Spirit. Cleansed of sin by his own acceptance of culpability and the Master's cauterizing insight, Peter's guilt-shriveled heart grew large enough to allow the Holy Spirit to do its work. The Spirit of Christ moved within him, moved him, and through his apostolic fervor would move other shriveled hearts to grow more supple, more conformable to the will and the work of God.

In each of our hearts, there is a hard diamond of self-realization waiting to catch and reflect the radiance of the Resurrection. The steady gaze of Christ, his insistent questions about our lifestyle and attitudes seek to uncover that truth and make us face up to it. Only when we admit our betrayals will we with Peter be able to accept the Master's commission. The lamp of life renewed probes our weakness, calls forth cleansing tears, heals our self-inflicted wounds, and then — praise the God of the living, not the dead — lights our way to the building up of the kingdom.

Three times he foreswore friendship on that
    faithless Thursday night.
Three times beside the sea he sought to put the
    matter right.
Three times he was absolved and given strength to bear
    the Light.

We await the kingdom, Lord, knowing that it will not touch the earth until our waiting becomes striving. We build the kingdom, Lord, aware that our faith is shifting sand. We witness the kingdom, Lord, assured that your loving mercy is our firm foundation.   Amen.

MONDAY OF THE THIRD WEEK

All together they confronted him, seized him, and led him off to the Sanhedrin. There they brought in false witnesses, who said: "This man never stops making statements against the holy place and the law. We have heard him claim that Jesus the Nazorean will destroy this place and change the customs which Moses handed down to us." The members of the Sanhedrin who sat there stared at him intently. Throughout, Stephen's face seemed like that of an angel (Acts 6:12-15).

Nicodemus was dismayed at the recent lack of decorum among the members of the Sanhedrin. It seemed that each time they met to discuss a matter pertaining to this Nazorean an atmosphere of agitation prevailed. The inattention of Caiaphas didn't help matters, either. Say what you might, in better days the High Priest's iron hand was a blessing when it came to restoring order. Lately, however, the man was no match for the feeling of frustration which swept over the Council each time a new disciple was brought forward. More than a few of his fellow Sadducees had expressed in Nicodemus' presence the desire to be rid of these "angels" once and for all. The rush to judgment during the last Passover had unnerved many who prided themselves on a fastidious adherence to legal process. That time they had given in to a certain laxity in procedure so as to dispose quickly of an imminent danger to the state. Now, false witnesses were again being paid on the grounds of expedience. Not that this Stephen with his outrageous accusations could be credible to any right-thinking person, but how many more of them might there be?

Most of our frustrations spring from the inability to direct our own lives, to see the happy conclusion of our plans. The passsenger who asks the cabbie to change a fifty dollar bill for a two mile trip, the hobo at the door who shatters Father's meditative mood: how many more thoughtless riders, how many more importunate beggars to stymie our well-prepared progress? How many more followers of this Galilean rabble-rouser will interrupt the good order of Jerusalem?

If you have a low frustration threshold, chances are that you are living in a very comfortable rut. The daily routine nurtures an artificial peace of mind, a forced continuum of predictable situations leaving no room for flexibility. Along comes the unexpected, the challenge of someone else's need, for example, and a prickly feeling of unease overtakes you. Unforeseen interruptions cause reason to short circuit; anger becomes the preferred reaction. Getting rid of the problem seems more important than solving it. It is easier to become enraged than engaged.

The roots of frustration lie in a specious source of well-being. When inner peace is based on the ego, it is a fragile structure indeed. It comes tumbling down every time you are crossed, every time your plan is superseded by the urgent plea of another. Peace springing from confidence in God, on the other hand, welcomes the introduction of another's need, for this peace depends not on the fulfillment of your plan, but on the divine plan, and God bends down to the luckless. The serenity of the saints stems from trust in Providence and a frank appraisal of the power of the ego. From the former comes a willingness to do God's work, from the latter a wariness of becoming self-engrossed. If God-centered Christians experience frustration, it is a holy impatience with their own egocentricity.

A good exercise to test your God-centeredness begins at the start of the day. Think of what you will probably be doing during the next eighteen hours. Then, from your experience, picture all the interruptions, especially those arising from the needs of others, which could frustrate your plans. If you can welcome them as opportunities to do the Lord's work in a new way, your peace of mind rests in the will of God. If, however, you side with the Sanhedrin and choose to get rid of the problems rather than solving them, you may find someday that you missed a chance to entertain an angel.

> Two graven dates, a bas-relief
> of cherubs mark a life as brief
> as lightning on that April day.
>
> A fault at birth, no matter whose,
> provoked the struggle he would lose
> as autumn staged her last display.
>
> His parents watched their summer dreams
> grow wintry as the doctors' schemes
> all ended with advice to pray.

Above the mossy stone each spring
two graying heads incline to bring
to life a memory and say:

We thank Thee, Lord, for in Thy care
an angel taught us how to share
and saved us from our selfish way.

Prince of Peace, bend down to us who seek serenity among the frustrations of daily life. Whisper the Father's will so that we may follow your example of trust and self-giving, and thus attain the quiet acceptance which you offered to all in need. Amen.

TUESDAY OF THE THIRD WEEK

The onlookers were shouting aloud, holding their hands over their ears as they did so. Then they rushed at him as one man, dragged him out of the city, and began to stone him. The witnesses meanwhile were piling their cloaks at the feet of a young man named Saul. As Stephen was being stoned he could be heard praying, "Lord Jesus, receive my spirit." He fell to his knees and cried out in a loud voice, "Lord, do not hold this sin against them." And with that he died   (Acts 7:57-60).

The second visit of Pope John Paul II to the United States was noteworthy for the variety of protesting voices which began to echo well before he left Rome. Unlike the 1979 visit which brought to our shores a newly elected and untested Pontiff, the 1987 trip promised a Pope with a track record of conservative leadership boldly stated. So concerned were the U.S. Bishops about his reception that they sent a delegation to the Vatican to urge him to soften what they assumed would be Papal pronouncements too gritty for American tastes. While there is merit in informing any visitor of the standard of behavior acceptable to a host, the Bishops' suggestions and John Paul's acceptance of them would have little bearing on the reaction of those whose attitudes toward a prophet of strict interpretation can be reduced to "Kill the messenger."

Many of us share the flaw seen in ancient kings as they struck down bearers of unpopular news. The runner who carried the tidings of victory twenty-two miles from Marathon to Athens received a hero's welcome; pity his poor counterpart who took the point of the sword as his reward for whispering to the Persians of their defeat. Pity the poor bathroom scale which gets a kick from the portly gentleman who just polished off a meal that would have shamed Henry VIII. Pity the poor mechanic whose ears ring with the invective of a driver who never bothered to add oil to his car's engine. Pity the poor teacher who reports failing grades to a classroom of vengeful underachievers. Bad news is seldom the doing or the desire of the messenger; often it is a result of our own machinations, yet we let our lightning strike the first available target. Pity process servers the world over.

In today's reading from the Acts of the Apostles, Stephen, the Deacon, in his indictment of the Jews who condemned Christ, foreshadowed among others Harry S Truman. "Why do you give the Republicans so much hell?" the crusty President was often asked. "I just tell the truth," he would reply, "and they think it's hell." In our daily lives, it doesn't take a revelation by the Holy Spirit to differentiate the messenger from the message. Simple patience and respect for the truth will show that the man or woman who informs us of the sad results of our own folly or of the mistakes of another cannot be held responsible. Rather than excoriate them, we should thank them for alerting us to a tear in the fabric of our lives. The messengers offer us a chance to mend the fraying tapestry. Indeed, healing sometimes hurts, but think of the alternative.

If anger is your usual reaction to the bearer of unwelcome news, there looms a greater danger than momentary loss of control. The ranks of those willing to tell you the truth will rapidly thin. When the word gets around that you will accept only good news, good news is all you will hear. Many a prince and many a pauper have been crushed by calamities foreseen by others who kept silent for fear of sword, stone, or spleen. Ask yourself today how you react to the truth that hurts. Do you stand in the crowd which dragged Stephen outside the city and raise the stone over your head? Do you sharpen your Persian sword as the runner approaches? Or do you see beyond the messenger to his message? Do you accept the hurt in hope of the healing?

> To the Bishop as he mounted
> for the first time to his throne
> bent the princely Consecrator
> with his confidential tone:
> Two things only in this office
> merit certainty, forsooth:
> Nevermore to pay for dinner.
> Nevermore to hear the truth.

Spirit of Truth, work in those who work with me. Make them bold enough to describe reality. Make me wise enough to receive them with humility. Amen.

WEDNESDAY OF THE THIRD WEEK

The members of the Church who had been dispersed went about preaching the word. Philip, for example, went down to the town of Samaria and there proclaimed the Messiah. Without exception, the crowds that heard Philip and saw the miracles he performed attended closely to what he had to say   (Acts 8:4-6).

To friends, Heather characterized her love for the new car as "almost sinful." She didn't tell them, however, that at night during that first month just before she got into bed, she would part the blinds and gaze at the brazen red coupe for half an hour sometimes. She also withheld a description of the traditional caress along its flanks each morning before driving to work. None of that would have gone over in the teacher's lounge at Roosevelt.

It was her first. She had paid too much, of course, but she didn't get taken. She got exactly what she wanted and signed the check for the down payment with a flourish. By the time she signed the second check, she was back on the bus again still buying a car that was no longer in the carport. The police had been very nice and let her cry as she consoled herself with the foggy notion that if there wasn't any car, there wouldn't be any notes. There would be, in fact, about a year of notes to bridge the insurance gap.

She chose not to take her old bus, the one that stopped almost in front of the apartment building; instead, she went toward the river three blocks to another line. Not that she didn't want her fellow teachers who were still bus-bound to know about the theft; she tearfully told them all the Monday after what she called the "kidnapping of Lady MacBuick."

She just hated to be back on the bus again, afraid she would say something hateful to a co-worker.

So she fell into the routine of walking three blocks and standing in front of St. Anne's, the church she had avoided since moving into the neighborhood. Except for weddings, she hadn't really been in any church since her second year at the U. Her mother hadn't stopped wringing her hands until she threatened not to come home for Christmas. Her father had little grounds for outrage.

The corner was pleasant enough until the first snow. Then, to save her slacks from the flying slush, she retreated to the narrow canopy over the scarred door. It was the blizzard — the third hundred-year blizzard in three years — that pushed her inside. The bus was not going to come and she couldn't see across the street.

Just like the church at home, she thought: blue votive lights flickering, garish statues in painful poses. The priest was at the altar rail speaking as she entered; she blushed when she realized he was speaking to her. She was the only one here because of the storm and could she come to the front pew and answer the prayers?

She didn't come back the following Sunday; these things take time. But by mid-December, she was again what her mother called "a practicing Catholic." She made sure in her own mind it wasn't just to please Mom or because of guilt feelings. It was too early to put her finger on it. Something about the roar of that storm and the quiet conversation of prayer and response and the warmth of the consecrated wine. Father G. helped too with his bachelor's breakfast and the snow tires on his Bronco.

That first day, after Father went on to the hospital, she had watched the snow from her window and tried to be professional about the whole thing. The barbed answers from Abnormal Psychology kept giving way to contentment, so she watched the snow and wondered how it happened.

Philip went to Samaria as a fugitive from Jerusalem. Paul boarded ship for Rome in chains. Peter ate the Gentiles' food because he was hungry. Heather was an orphan in the storm.

What is your story? How did it happen?

> Limpid dissertations and pellucid postulates
> proving God exists in philosophical debates
> fail to form the circumstance
>   which destiny awaits.
>
> Knowing how insistent is the stimulus of need
> God the Mother of invention moves to supersede
> logic with necessity
>   a light to kindly lead.

Almighty God, I am ashamed to admit my fear of adversity. I will not ask for even a moment's misfortune, but I know it will come without my bidding. May I be consoled in times of trouble with the confidence that you can bring good out of any evil.   Amen.

THURSDAY OF THE THIRD WEEK

It happened that an Ethiopian eunuch, a court official in charge of the entire treasury of Candace (a name meaning queen) of the Ethiopians, had come on a pilgrimage to Jerusalem and was returning home. He was sitting in his carriage reading the prophet Isaiah. The Spirit said to Philip, "Go and catch up with that carriage." Philip ran ahead and heard the man reading the prophet Isaiah. He said to him. "Do you really grasp what you are reading?"

Thursday of the Third Week

"How can I," the man replied, "unless someone explains it to me?" With that, he invited Philip to get in and sit down beside him. Philip launched out with this Scripture passage as his starting point, telling him the good news of Jesus   (Acts 8:27-31, 35).

Bible readers can understand the frustration of the Ethiopian eunuch. Where is the certainty that my interpretation of a certain passage of Scripture is superior to yours? Today's unrestrained and well-publicized Bible Wars among Scripture scholars of every stripe generate more heat than light, breed more confusion than confidence. Arguments once barely murmured in the hushed groves of academe now resound in the pews and divide living Churches. In our own Church, Papal pronouncements meant for scholars have found their way to widely-read Conciliar documents which stress the necessity of recognizing different literary styles used by the inspired authors. The Dogmatic Constitution on Divine Revelation of Vatican Council II advises the Bible reader as well as the scholar that truth is expressed in many ways, that Scripture contains varied and quite distinct forms of literature, and that the ancients perceived reality differently than we do (See *Dei Verbum*, Chapter III). Biblical scholarship is encouraged, but to assure the non-scholar that the center will hold despite professorial musings, the Council Fathers reiterate the traditional teaching that definitive interpretation is reserved to the Church under the guidance of the Holy Spirit.

This is all as it should be. Yet, twenty-five years beyond the Council, Tony with the Bible on his lap after a punishing day at the plant remains perplexed. Being a thorough footnote and Introduction reader, he has come to accept the difference in style between the Book of Genesis and Luke's Gospel. What worries Tony is this: If the holy writers were so free and easy with details in order to make a spiritual point, how can anyone be certain of what is really important? For instance, do the angel's words to Mary command the same certitude as those of Jesus at the institution of the Eucharist? And when Tony hears that there are varying literary styles even within a single book of the Bible, even within a Gospel — the story of Jesus, he is apt to close his Bible with a snap and turn on "Dallas." At least he knows when the Ewings are embellishing the truth.

In the Acts of the Apostles, we never hear the details of the lesson in Scriptural interpretation which Philip teaches the Ethiopian eunuch. But one phrase assures us that he would tell Tony the same thing had he overtaken him at a stoplight on the way home from work. He would tell him "the good news of Jesus." The good news of Jesus transcends literary styles and archaic modes of perceiving reality. The good news of Jesus still amazes the scholars who pore over dusty tomes. The good news of Jesus is why we read the Bible. The good news came first.

If you are confused about the treasure house of Scripture which Vatican Council II unlocked, remember Jesus came first. His Incarnation was foretold in an Old Testament filled with apparent contradictions and celebrated in a New Testament comprised of differing viewpoints and styles. You, with your viewpoint, write the Bible every time you read it. You write it on your heart as a blessing for today, your day. The word of God come to fragile life on printed pages only partially reveals the Living Word whose enfleshment is the Church. The Bible is the Church speaking to you. Its words are imprecise tools which many authors have used in an attempt to express the fullness of God's revelation to humankind; they must be measured against the teaching of the Church just as surely as the Ethiopian eunuch's unformed interpretation of

Isaiah had to be held up to the bright light of the explanation of the Church's messenger, Philip. To be confused about the Bible is not unusual, but to ignore the enlightenment offered by the Spirit of Christ in his Church is, at the least, foolhardy.

Resolve to continue or resume regular reading of Scripture. Nowhere will you find a word so beneficial to your spiritual life. Thanks to the inspiration of the Holy Spirit, nowhere will you find a description of God's love which conforms so closely to the truth. Learn to accept apparent contradictions as they arise, but don't be content with them. In Bible commentaries and Scripture seminars, seek the clarifying word of the Church which gave birth to the Bible and still nurtures it for the life of the world.

>   Tugging
>   thumping
>   pinching
>   fingers span the vast expanse of pachydermis.
>   Calling
>   gasping
>   shouting
>   voices list the mysteries for sightless seekers
>   probing
>   testing
>   finding
>   proof of hose piano rope and peasant hovel.
>   Flinching
>   snorting
>   waving
>   tusk and trunk he lumbers toward his jungle haven.

Spirit of Wisdom, lead us aright through the words you made holy. Help us to comprehend the story of our salvation. And when we are confused, satisfy us with the peace that passes understanding. Amen.

FRIDAY OF THE THIRD WEEK

> The Jews quarreled among themselves, saying, "How can he give us his flesh to eat?" Thereupon Jesus said to them: "Let me solemnly assure you, if you do not eat the flesh of the Son of Man and drink his blood, you have no life in you"   (John 6:52-53).

Some of the most shameful episodes in the history of Christianity have been the result of the identification of Jews as Christ-killers. Abrogation of civil-rights, wholesale deportations, and genocide have been ordered by tyrants and condoned by common folk. Fifty years ago, the citizens of the most advanced nation in Europe allowed their leaders to carry out a "final solution" which resulted in the deaths of three to six million Jews. As in all pogroms, the pretexts were nativistic; Abraham's spawn were undemocratic, cosmopolitan, subversive. Fundamental to the racist propaganda which fueled the Holocaust was the tacit permission granted by the timidity of many churches. It was not necessary to be too fastidious in protecting the rights of those whose lineage bore the stain of Christ's spilled blood.

Today's Gospel passage forces the thoughtful Christian to ponder a disturbing question, a question which should lead to healing. How could the majority of Jews of Jesus' day have done otherwise than turn their backs on a man who made such outrageous claims?

Suppose you were a Jew of that time. You practiced your faith, obeyed the authorities, and like many were caught up in the expectation of the imminent appearance of the Messiah. You had heard this Jesus speak several times. He said so many beautiful and encouraging things about the poor in spirit, about the loving mercy of Yahweh, about the coming of the kingdom. True, some of his words and deeds were hard to take. He attacked your religious leaders, honored tax collectors and prostitutes with his presence, usurped the divine prerogative of forgiving sins. His prophecy about destroying and rebuilding the Temple gave you the shivers, but to be in his presence even across a great crowd made you feel good about yourself. Then came the day of reckoning.

"If you do not eat the flesh of the Son of Man and drink his blood, you have no life in you." He went too far. You were ready to entertain the idea that he might fulfill some very important prophecies, but his deliberate words about eating flesh allowed no hint of poetry or symbolism. You kept waiting for him to explain that he was referring to the Paschal Lamb of which your people devoutly partook each year, but that clarification never came. Rather, this Galilean insisted that eating his flesh was the part you would play in the revelation of his Sonship. You and many of your friends could walk no longer with him.

For centuries, the Jewish people have stood condemned for the same judgment you and I would have rendered against such a provocative visionary. In recent times, we have become accustomed to the Church's new emphasis on the Jewish question which stresses that only a small group of leaders was to blame for the crucifixion. Such a reappraisal makes eminent sense, but there is work to be done down deep where racial memories bubble. A good remedy for the sickness of stereotyping lies in role-playing. Reread today's Scripture passage and be a Jew listening to a man inviting you to eat his flesh. Should your "No" condemn you to suffer from two thousand years of prejudice?

> We beat our breasts in sixty-three
> and said we all killed Kennedy.
> The nation gorged itself on guilt,
> wept over walls that hate had built
> between religion, class, and race.
> We were the tears on Lincoln's face.
>
> We sobered up in sixty-four
> and showed collective blame the door.
> A people came to see the fact
> that from a madman's lonely act
> flows no indictment of his kind.
> There are some ties that do not bind.

Lord of all, save us from the sin of prejudice. May we strive to recognize the worth of each individual. Keep us from rejecting whole groups and classes because of the folly of a few, as we recall that like Judas and Caiaphas, you too were a Jew.   Amen.

SATURDAY OF THE THIRD WEEK

> From this time on, many of his disciples broke away and would not remain in his company any longer. Jesus then said to the Twelve, "Do you want to leave me too?" Simon Peter answered him, "Lord, to whom shall we go? You have the words of eternal life. We have come to believe; we are convinced that you are God's holy one"   (John 6:66-69).

Every Sunday morning, Victor goes to the fitness center for a workout. In the beginning, it was an escape from his parents who ordered him to church. Later, he fled to the barbells and weights when his wife nagged him about the Lord's day. Now, he fancies it a kind of worship, a sweaty prayer of thanks to God for the gift of his body.

Thursday nights find Marge with her encounter group. Her psychiatrist had originally prescribed the sessions as part of an anti-paranoia therapy. Since those first painful confrontations, she has decided that she is closest to the divine mind when she hears the stories which pour forth from her more unfortunate companions.

Helene puts on Debussy, draws the drapes, and spends Saturday afternoons thinking pleasant thoughts, letting the mood of the music carry her to a higher plane. Sometimes she glimpses heaven, a place not unlike the grove of mountain pines she discovered on a hike in her teens.

Ned paints. Miguel runs. Evelyn works the soil in her garden. Each engages in a well-intentioned pursuit of a lofty essence, an extra-terrestrial serenity. Each substitutes private striving for participation in a worshipping assembly. Each is ultimately misguided.

St. Peter said, "Lord, to *whom* shall we go?", and thereby raised a personal pronoun to spiritual prominence. It was the person of Jesus that bound Peter and the others to him. Not power or wealth, therefore, but only another human being could compete with Jesus for the affection of his followers. The Twelve had decided that the words of eternal life were heard on the lips of only one person, the charismatic rabbi from Nazareth.

The competition, the person who always draws you and me away from Jesus has a name easy to remember: "I." Whether it is my ideal self reflected in a composer's work, or my injured self soothed by the trauma of others, or my perfected self seen in the gymnasium mirror, the *whom* to which I go bears my name.

Many avoid common worship or attend grudgingly because at a gathering of authentic praise, the self is subsumed in community. The songs, the prayers, the preaching all require the sacrifice called participation. The best liturgies are those which stimulate a giving-over of the self to fellow celebrants and, in the end, to the Lord. Granted, these peak worship experiences are not always possible; the blame for boredom usually lies with those who withhold themselves from full participation.

When you want to be in communion with the Lord, to whom do you go? Is it often to your self? If so, you may be blaming God erroneously for dryness in prayer and lack of consolation. In seeking the cause of spiritual aridity, look first to your approach to community worship. The Fathers of the Council knew the power of the self and, thus, emphasized the effective counter-force. "The liturgy is the summit toward which the activity of the Church is directed; at the same time it is the fountain from which all her power flows" (Constitution on the Sacred Liturgy, No. 10). Those who regularly pray or meditate alone cannot know the person of Christ unless their solitary actions are a preparation for or the result of an assembly of praise. The words of eternal life must be heard on human lips if a worshipper is to be in communion with the living Lord. The self must be sacrificed to the worshipping community if the Christian is to be united with Christ, the man of sacrifice. To *whom* shall you go, your self or the Lord?

> Together
> in the streaming beams of a rose window
> stand the summoned
> flecked with iridescence
> > a people
> > > as disparate as the shattered spectrum of their mantle.

God
with his thousand-faceted eye
sees beforeafterinto
   gray of illness
      blue despair
         crystal innocence
            hope ever green
               and in this house of glass
                  confects a rainbow.

Father of light, in our midst you placed the lamp of life renewed. May its glow sparkle in the eyes of the people you have gathered and bathe the world in Sonshine.   Amen.

FOURTH SUNDAY OF EASTER

Jesus said:
   "I am the good shepherd.
   I know my sheep
   and my sheep know me
   in the same way that the Father knows me
   and I know the Father;
   for these sheep I will give my life" (John 10:14-15).

Even to this day, the rural villages of Palestine have on their perimeters one or more common sheepfolds. In the blazing evening, squinting shepherds shuffle beside their bleating flocks urging them toward large pens, there to mingle with other herds under the watchful eye of a night keeper. In the morning, the veteran herdsman does not rely on brands or ear tags in assembling his charges; he simply stands and calls, and from the mingled flocks step forward his own. They recognize his voice. Despite the fact that all the shepherds are calling at the same time, each sheep knows his master's inimitable blend of urgency and affection.

When John's Gospel reports that the good shepherd and his sheep know each other, the knowledge referred to transcends the narrow definition of the act of perception. The words of Jesus mean that he is personally involved with those who answer his call. His involvement is much deeper than simple awareness of the needs of his flock; Jesus is not merely a detached observer of the human scene. He is an intimate of those he was sent to save in a way similar to that of his intimacy with his heavenly Father. Jesus' affection for his people partakes of the mutual love animating the Holy Trinity. And, says the good shepherd, "my sheep know me" in the same way. All of us who are privileged to number ourselves among his flock are graced at least with the potential for personal involvement with him. The slow, sometimes painful realization of that potential is the process known as spiritual growth. The testing, or proving of that potential in prayer is the part of spiritual growth called discernment.

At the age of eight-and-a-half, little Billy is quite aware that his mother knows his name. He and she are mutually involved in the kaleidoscope of feelings which invest life. Although she never calls him anything but "Billy," his response depends on whether she is demanding that he explain his report card or inviting him to a good-night hug. That single diminutive can warn of exasperation or shock, warm with compassion or forgiveness. It is a shepherd calling her lamb to involvement in growth. The lamb must discern the circumstance and make a response which will sustain mutual love. As he grows older, Billy may respond inappropriately and strain the bonds of affection, but his mother stands ready to right his wrongs and repair the relationship.

In today's Gospel, the good shepherd acknowledges the possibility of radical damage to our personal involvement with him. Depending on the gravity of our betrayal, we can even sever our ties to Christ, at least from our point of view. He stands ready to repair the damage. So important is the relationship that he pledges to give his life to renew the bonds of love shattered by sin. It is this pledge that we discern in his voice, this promise of healing we rely on when our spiritual growth is stymied or reversed. The good shepherd never culls us out of his flock. When we wander in the wilderness, he leaves the other ninety-nine in order to seek us out. Even in the dark night, he calls to us, and because of our history of involvement with him, we know his voice.

Growth and discernment, involvement and listening is the work of the flock. Involvement means gathering with our brothers and sisters around the Book and the Table; discernment means honing our spiritual sensitivity in solitary prayer. In the silence of the sheepcote at night, we are left to our own thoughts. The silence used rightly is a time of remembering the intonations of solace, forgiveness, and hope in the voice of the shepherd. In the morning, the call takes flesh in the invitation to gather with the shepherd to be led to verdant pastures and restful waters.

Go to your sheepfold, your prayer place this evening. As the light dies, recall the voice of the shepherd as it has come to you so many times. In various inflections, it tells the history of your relationship with him. The theme of the story is love, an echo of the eternal call which draws Son to Father and Father to Son in the Spirit. Tomorrow, the invitation will take flesh again as the shepherd stands at the gate to urge you to step into another day, into another celebration of intimacy. Have no fear. You know the voice. It is he who gave his life for his flock.

> Father, Son, and Holy Spirit
> bend to one another
> silent in their cosmic discourse
> but for Christ, our brother.
>
> Came the shepherd to reveal this
> wondrous affirmation:
> Calling each of us by name is
> heaven's conversation.

Good Shepherd, help us to hear your voice amid the noisy demands of our day. Call us to gather with your flock and sing with you the praise of our Father.   Amen.

MONDAY OF THE FOURTH WEEK

Peter said:
> "Then I remembered what the Lord had said: 'John baptized with water but you will be baptized with the Holy Spirit.' If God was giving them the same gift he gave us when we first believed in the Lord Jesus Christ, who was I to interfere with him?"
> (Acts 11:16-17).

By the end of the sixth telephone call, Dr. Hubbard's simmering exasperation had bubbled over. He went for a walk to cool off. All six had turned him down, mainline denominations with imposing buildings and rock solid congregations which included most of his golfing partners. Each minister had put it differently, but the verdict was always the same: No provision for burying a John Doe.

As a small-town medical examiner, he had dealt with only a few unidentified fatals. Chief Irwin was always able to unearth a family connection. It might take a week or two; a few calls to the State Police about laundry labels or birthmarks resulted in someone with ill-fitting Sunday clothes stepping off the Greyhound to ask grudgingly about procedures and costs. Sometimes the doctor would chip in for shipping just to close the file. This time five weeks had gone by with the old tramp still in the cold room. Although Hubbard was a devout agnostic, he squelched the Chief's suggestion about taking up a collection at the Courthouse to send the body to the Capital City coroner. "We've got plenty of cemeteries here," he had said. "Let one of the churches take care of it." He hadn't considered the question of affiliation. It took six calls to learn what he already knew. This John Doe wasn't on anybody's rolls.

Three blocks from the hospital stood a weatherbeaten clapboard building from which issued on this Wednesday evening the sounds of clapping hands and hoarse Amens. He had never noticed the peeling sign before: "Holy Tabernacle of God, Universal." As he waited on the opposite curb, the doors opened and beaming worshippers poured out, if forty people can be said to pour. Hugs and handclasps and backslaps and more Amens, then the Pastor was alone, sweat glistening on her black forehead. Dr. Hubbard crossed the street.

On Saturday morning, a professional doubter sat in the last pew of a pet store-turned-temple and felt confirmed in his thirty-year resolve to stay away from churches. His resistance to emotional rhetoric and anointed earnestness was as strong as ever. He paid little attention to the

Reverend Dorothy Williams' roller coaster sermon until she repeated for the congregation what she had told him on Wednesday night. "We are glad to lift up our brother, John, and send him across the river because it is God's work, and when we do God's work, we are sanctified in the Holy Ghost." He looked at the pine box, the wreath, and the ladies in white who would slowstep to their cemetery. God's work? Well, somebody's work. For today, anyway, he could believe a little . . . as long as it didn't require going to church.

In our passage from the Acts of the Apostles, God moves ahead of his Church. This can be disconcerting to those of us who believe that he is locked up securely in traditional doctrine and orthodox practice. We are so comfortable with the unvarying rhythms of our faith that we can overlook or, indeed, look away from the man in the ditch. Nothing less than a vision from heaven could make St. Peter break free of the strictures of the faith of his Fathers. Think today of the vision God sent you when your religion became a strait jacket. Probably not a canvas dropped from heaven containing beasts and birds, more likely a man in a ditch.

> At moments least predictable
> the rootless make their plea
> for neither home nor steady job
> but mere identity.
> The alms required is certainty
> that in some reckless flight
> there was not lost what made them real
> back somewhere in the night.
> Against our patience rub the strayed
> like cat upon a leg;
> content with kick or brief caress
> a sign is all they beg
> a curt admission that they are
> have been and will be yet.
> For if the blessed mark their souls
> then God will not forget.

Lord, Guide of our lives, lead us on our pilgrim way. If we stray, pull us back. If we stumble, steady us. If we fall, forgive us. And if we come upon a lost brother or sister, strengthen our sense of direction. Amen.

TUESDAY OF THE FOURTH WEEK

Jesus said:
> "My sheep hear my voice.
> I know them,
> and they follow me.
> I give them eternal life,
> and they shall never perish.
> No one shall ever snatch them
>   out of my hand.
> My Father is greater than all,
>   in what he has given me,
> and there is no snatching
>   out of his hand.
> The Father and I are one" (John 10:27-30).

Last Friday, we held the lamp of new life over the crowds who sought to hear from the lips of Jesus some confirmation that the age-old promises made to the Chosen People were beginning to take flesh. In the bright beam of truth, we saw would-be followers turn away, not because the flesh was that of Jesus, but because he would have them eat the flesh of the promise. It was too much to be asked, too indelicate to consider, too far from the mainstream of Jewish thought and tolerance. Still, they left him reluctantly, for his charism was like a magnet among iron filings.

The reaction to Jesus' words in today's Gospel is quite different, not a polite leave-taking but the threat of violence from both legalists and renegades. The former are scandalized at Jesus' claim to unity with Yahweh; the latter are frustrated to the point of rage that the one who seemed to have the best chance of uniting the people for revolution turns out to be an unacceptable visionary. Insults are hurled and stones are about to be . . . all because of a little red *hen*.

A few verses earlier, the hide-bound and zealots alike complain about what they perceive as Jesus' evasiveness in the face of urgent, essential questions. "How long are you going to keep us in suspense? If you really are the Messiah, tell us so in plain words" (John 10:24). Nothing is more plain than the *hen* which Jesus uses to make clear his relationship with his heavenly Father. *Hen* in the Greek of John's Gospel means *one thing*. In the present translation, Jesus says of his relationship with his Father: "The Father and I are *one*." He could have said: "The Father and I are *at one*" or "*of one mind*" or "*in agreement* on everything." He chose instead to say to the Jews, the archetypical monotheists, that "the Father and I are *hen* (one thing)." *Of one mind* or *in agreement* would have offered those in either camp who wanted to stay with him a convenient reason for shouting down those with stones in their hands. After all, anyone who claims to be the Messiah was expected to say he is in agreement with Yahweh. But to equate himself with the Most High is blasphemy to the powers-that-be and renunciation of the role of rebel chieftain to those who chafed at collaboration with the Romans: a classic no-win situation. When Jesus uses that little red *hen* to claim a unity of being with the divine mind, will, and operation, he deliberately introduces another of those hard sayings which so infuriated both sides. For saying he is God, a man can legally be stoned. By this time, there are few left to shout down the law. Jesus must slip away.

In the midst of a people who bind themselves so enthusiastically to the material world, modern Christians give too little notice to their own surrender to a strictly humanistic idea of Christ. So pervasive, so insistent is the description of Jesus as a common man, proletarian hero and liberator that the aspect of his divinity becomes something of an irritant: God, after all, is out there, and we live here. The Son of God is someone we shall meet in heaven, if there is a heaven. It is better to build heaven on this earth just in case we have misread the Gospels. Jesus can be our model in any case. His antiestablishmentarian teachings and revolutionary fervor can inspire every endeavor from slum clearance to the violent overthrow of a dictatorship. When you paint Jesus, put a rifle in his hand.

Meditate today on the inexorable ticking of a clock. Each second brings this world one step closer to nonexistence. All will turn to dust and even the dust will be annihilated. Rather than a dream of heaven on earth, authentic faith offers the promise of a haven when the universe is swept away. The friends of God will be caught up to meet his divine Son, Christ, the King. If you must paint Jesus storming the barricades, place at his heel a little red *hen.*

> The measure of belief
> is the sweat it brings to life
> wrung from sinews stretching to
> stem the rising tide of strife
> sprung from facile rationales —
> here enshrine the out-of-date,
> there prescribe anarchic change —
> which faith must moderate.

Heavenly Father, the place you have prepared for us seems so far away and the kingdom we have built so fragile. Give us the faith to see that what begins slowly here will come to perfection hereafter. Amen.

WEDNESDAY OF THE FOURTH WEEK

Jesus proclaimed aloud:
"If anyone hears my words
  and does not keep them,
I am not the one to condemn him,
for I did not come to condemn the world
but to save it.
Whoever rejects me and does not
  accept my words
already has his judge,
namely, the word I have spoken —
it is that which will condemn him
  on the last day"   (John 12:47-48).

Lately, fast food shops have become more accommodating. A gastronomic evolution has occurred in the matter of choice. When once the consuming populace was pleasantly amazed by mere speed — giving the order, receiving the burger, and gulping it down all in a matter of fifteen minutes, now the national chains have taken a lettuce leaf from the humble cafeteria. Options have multiplied exponentially to the point where the trip to the salad bar, beverage counter, and dessert table takes longer than the ingestion of their bounty.

Since grace follows nature, choice has also become popular in the churches. Cafeteria Christians decide which doctrines they can digest and which give them soulburn, which need only a bit of seasoning and which must be disguised under a sauce of exceptions. Unfortunately for the consumer of pop tart theology, Jesus stands in the shadow of the cross rather then under the golden arches.

"Whoever rejects me and does not accept my words, already has his judge," namely, the word or that part of the word he rejected. Jesus says we must take him whole; we cannot pick and choose between the comfortable and the sacrificial. Yet, it is not he who will condemn us for removing the bitter herbs from his message. He doesn't have to. The word itself will be our judge. If we are on a diet of sugar and mush, our spirit will lose its tone. If we avoid the nourishment provided by the grit and struggle of sacrifice, the world will pin us two falls out of three.

No one reading this book can say that he or she finds every one of Jesus' words palatable. Nor do the Church's interpretations of his teachings all go down with equal ease. The fact remains that the banquet table of the Lord is not a cafeteria line; the more we partake of only what we like, the greater the risk of spiritual weakness. When Jesus says that his word "will condemn him on the last day," he is speaking of the whole menu. One cannot reach the heavenly banquet without the soul food which gives strength for the journey.

Review your spiritual menu this day. Does it consist of the entire word of Jesus and the traditions of the Church he founded to nurture his people? If not, if you are picky about what you choose to believe, you may be on a starvation diet. Take some bitter herbs along with the lamb. They may be hard to swallow, but the sting will strengthen you.

To spark the world's beginning, a Godly rumination
made matter out of nothing but love's pronunciation.
This Word of life provided the pattern of creation,
especially for children of human generation.
In time, the scourge of pride did invite annihilation,
until the Father's mercy became the Incarnation.
The Holy Spirit lingered to seal the world's salvation
and tell the joyous news of its reconciliation.

Can I be deaf by choice to some thorny declaration
and honestly take part in this saving conversation?

Spirit of Wisdom, I need not know everything. Keep from me the trajectory of the lightning and the boundaries of the abyss. Rather, fill this earthen vessel with simple faith amid a universe of mysteries, with childlike hope against the unknown future, and with quiet love for your holy truths.   Amen.

THURSDAY OF THE FOURTH WEEK

[After Jesus had washed the feet of the disciples
he said:]
"I solemnly assure you,
no slave is greater than his master,
no messenger outranks the one who sent him.
Once you know all these things,
blest will you be
if you put them into practice"   (John 13:16-17).

Success: America's engine, green light across the water, hope of every father for his son. The polestar of success stands cities on their sides, stacking to the skies cubicles tense with the electricity of gain. The sweet smell of success is a heady perfume for those who must prove their own worth. Few are exempt from the dream. Even those who have heaped upon themselves the rewards of accomplishment find their thirst building anew, for worldly success contains within itself this deadly irony: Although victory often depends on using others, it is at the same time the gift of others. One cannot declare himself or herself successful and there rest content. Tomorrow the gift may be withdrawn and bestowed upon a more dedicated striver, a less contented dreamer.

In the crannies of our society lurk those who have left the playing field. They do not hold with contemporary ideas of success. Among these are the monks, the men in vows who rely upon one another but succumb only to God. Starchasers and truth-seekers, they take the teachings and example of the Wounded Healer and make of them a life stretching from *Benedicamus Domino* to *Requiescat in pace*.

Every monastery, no matter how well-protected by the world's indifference, has a doorkeeper. His task is to prevent success from crooning to the candle-holders and lamplighters who live in eight-by-twelve cells. A monk's existence hinges on the guarantee that he will be unsuccessful so that God's will may be done. What else might be expected from a man who takes a vow of foolishness? Without a hint of triumph, he looks to the final judgment, a judgment which will be an invitation extended only to fools.

"No slave is greater than his master, no messenger outranks the one who sent him." A monk must fail because Jesus failed. There came a dark Friday afternoon when, in the estimation of his countrymen, of the leaders of his religion, even of his closest followers, the cross was the pulpit of a fool who said too much during his life and not enough at the end. No monk wishes to rise higher than the cross. In the desert after his baptism, Jesus turned back the devil's offer of easy victory, another in a lifetime of skirmishes which ended with his refusal to "take yourself down from the cross." The monk seeks his own desert, taking on the coloration of the blowing sand, making himself invisible to the searching eye of accomplishment. He becomes transparent in order that the Master's example of humble service might shine through him. He embraces as his creed the words of St. Paul to the Galatians: "I have been crucified with Christ, and the life I live now is not my own; Christ is living in me" (2:19-20).

Not everyone should be a monk, but each of us should know one. When our drive for success blinds us to the dignity of others, when the urge to exploit replaces human respect and, in the act of forcing our brothers and sisters to serve us, we become slaves to success, we need to visit a monastery. They are by design not easy to find, but the search is worth it. Whom the doorkeeper finds for you isn't important; any son of the desert will do. In a simple room, you will hear wisdom singing and see her radiance. The Master's commission will come alive in a transparent man. "As I have done, so you must do." Don't step on feet, wash them.

worn by
divine endeavor
Spirit seeking foothold
in a tiny cell
lights upon a tonsure
anod with thoughts of
elsewhere

dream they
of gondolas in
Venice slipping past the
Sphinx as native girls
Turkey trot on rocky
Gibraltar bathed in
moonlight

monk and
reposing Spirit
cling to blessed languor
pleased to tarry while
heavenly insistence
beseeches both to
mission

Risen Lord, you lay three days in the tomb while news of your failure echoed through Jerusalem. Permit me to rest in you away from the pressures of wordly accomplishment until the hour of true victory in heaven. Amen.

FRIDAY OF THE FOURTH WEEK

"You know the way that leads
where I go."
"Lord," said Thomas, "we do not know
where you are going. How can we
know the way?" Jesus told him:
"I am the way, and the truth, and the life;
no one comes to the Father
but through me"   (John 14:4-6).

No one was surprised when Ida Zerwinski announced her imminent demise. She had a reputation for that sort of thing. Jesus had been appearing to her at intervals ever since Ignace fell on the beach at Anzio. She knew he was dead a week before the War Department telegram arrived. Jesus had revealed it to her while she was making bandages with the Sodality on a blustery January evening in 1944. The other ladies heard the wind rattling the door; Aunt Ida heard the Lord with bad news about her husband.

Then she began to see him. One day as she searched for an old prayer book in the storeroom above the garage, Jesus stood next to a dress form and told her the war would soon be over, but that the President wouldn't live to see it. Subsequent revelations were not confined to matters of life and death. The Savior correctly predicted the victor in every presidential race but one from 1948 on. He missed in 1960, probably because everybody knew a Catholic couldn't win. Despite the cool logic of a succession of newly-ordained assistant priests, parishioners of Ida's generation regularly came to her for a glimpse of the future or a plea for intercession. Each left a picture of Jesus on which she would scrawl a pertinent note to herself. Although the younger members of the Sodality made fun of such superstitious gullibility, she never tempered her announcements at the meetings. Toward the end, however, even her closest friends pretended to giggle along with sophisticates.

In March, 1964, Father Spelchek brought her final revelation to the Monsignor. She had told the ladies during refreshments that the twelve-year old Jesus had spoken to her from the circle of wise men in the Temple. He was calling her home to be with Ignace and President Kennedy. The Monsignor inquired as to the location of this vision. "In the garage," said Father, "while she was putting away the rock salt." The Monsignor didn't lift his head from the breviary, "Then she'll be dead in a month. She's never been wrong in the garage."

At the covered dish dinner in the church basement after the funeral, Monsignor Kurkolski regaled the crowd with his patented stories of the old country. He told two on Aunt Ida with whom he had attended primary school in Cracow. Even then, she had predicted he would be a priest. (She had said "bishop," but he kept that to himself.) Father Spelchek slipped across the street and found that the side door of Aunt Ida's garage was unlocked. Up in the storeroom, the pictures were tacked to the walls, maybe seventy of them, large and small pious fancies of what the Son of God looked like. All of them bore a few words in Polish, Aunt Ida's reminder of the donor's question or petition. "Will my daughter get better?" "When will the factory reopen?" "Lord have mercy on the soul of Karol Grabowski." A magazine cover caught his eye: Jesus in a chasuble with Aunt Ida's note, "When will my mother be allowed to emigrate?" The publication date made it only three weeks old. He had assured himself that sophistication and ridicule had put an end to these superstitions long ago. But no, there was last year's Sacred Heart calendar. In fact, it seemed over half the pictures were of recent vintage with no curling edges, no yellowed borders, and all annotated in Ida's spidery hand.

That evening, the Monsignor confirmed his assistant's fears. The grandmas and grandpas kept going to Aunt Ida until the day of her death. Indeed, there was sort of a run on the garage after her final prediction. "Don't be too hard on them, Leo. God can seem so far away and Ida was just down the block." On another day, Father Spelchek would have trotted out his theological arguments about the inevitable despair which superstition breeds, his own experience of the strength required and given in a pure, uncluttered relationship with the Lord, and his hopes that the Bishops meeting in Rome might put in their proper place sacramentals and apparitions and pious cults. He held his tongue this time, remembering that the picture of Jesus in a chasuble which he saw in Aunt Ida's garage this morning was from the cover of this month's *Priest* magazine. He knew his copy lay on his bed table, intact.

> Each sand-plumed dune the nomads pass
> increases distance from
> oases drenched in green and gold
> whence desert migrants come.
>
> Ahead dust-borne mirages sing
> of succulents and shade
> until a stumbling step reveals
> another hope delayed.
>
> So desiccated is the life
> and treacherous the way
> an errant pilgrimage where truth
> seems only to betray.
>
> Thrice-fooled the purblind plodders push
> their rescuer aside
> that hope become incarnate sent
> to be both goal and guide.

Holy Spirit of Truth, lead us away from the path of superstition. Purify our prayers. Enlighten our devotions. Confirm our reasoned hopes. May we trust not in worldly fancies but in the love of God revealed in Jesus Christ, our Lord.   Amen.

SATURDAY OF THE FOURTH WEEK

> Jesus said to his disciples:
> "I solemnly assure you,
> the man who has faith in me
> will do the works I do,
> and greater far than these.
> Why? Because I go to the Father,
> and whatever you ask in my name
> I will do,
> so as to glorify the Father in the Son.
> Anything you ask me in my name
> I will do"   (John 14:12-14).

Bedraggled children stand in front of their roofless home while the camera lingers on a mother's tears. Her story has been told many times in this devastated neighborhood since the tornado hopscotched across the eastern suburbs before dawn this morning. Noise like a freight train. Family huddled in the basement. Sounds of wood splintering and tearing. And invariably: "I asked the good Lord to save us. He sure must have been listening."

A badly frightened homemaker can be pardoned for the popular misconception of prayer which her words betray. It can be heard after any calamity. "We prayed to the Lord for rescue. He changed the course of nature to protect us." There is great merit in praying for salvation of any kind if it is understood that the most efficacious of blessings granted are those realized within rather than outside the soul. As St. Augustine says in his letter to Proba, "We need to use words (of prayer) so that we may remind ourselves to consider carefully what we are asking, not so that we may think we can instruct the Lord or prevail on him." As for the gratitude expressed by the woman over God's attentiveness, Augustine goes on to assure all petitioners that God knows the needs of his children before they are lifted up to him in words. Authentic prayer is never a means of getting God's ear or changing God's mind; rather, it is a process of conforming the petitioner's will to the plan of God.

Prayer is a dialogue. God's work in the dialogue is not to make a hundred adjustments in the intersection of nature and circumstance in order to keep the tornado from hitting the house. God's work is to move the soul of the petitioner to acceptance of his will. The petitioner's work is to be open to that movement. This openness is the asking "in my name" of which Jesus speaks in today's Gospel passage. The name of Jesus is by no means some magic formula guaranteed to alter God's disposition. This kind of mistake in prayer leads people to all kinds of aberrations covering the spectrum from prayers "never known to fail" to the penchant of benighted members of some religious sects for handling poisonous snakes. The use of the name of Jesus as a password will not rescue the foolish no matter how sincere or desperate they may be.

"Anything you ask in my name I will do." To the Jews of Jesus' time, one's name was equivalent to one's person. What Jesus meant was this: If you ask something of me and you are in communion with me, you shall have it. Therefore, authentic prayer is that offered by a petitioner who has the mind of Christ, that is, the obedience to the Father's will expressed in the Garden of Gethsemane. Prayer in the name of Jesus is prayer which has as its principle the acceptance of God's will in any situation including the most desperate. This is the prayer of which Augustine speaks, the prayer that is preparation for the movement of God in the soul. Every prayer in Jesus' name is a statement of belief that his Father wants only the best for his children. That was the guiding principle of Jesus' mission on earth. If we are to be in communion with him, if we are to have the mind of the Master, we must pray in his name that our Father's will be done in us and in those for whom we pray.

Today, take steps to purify your practice of prayer. Open yourself to the movement of God, the working of his Holy Spirit in your life. "The Spirit too helps us in our weakness, for we do not know how to pray as we ought; but the Spirit himself makes intercession for us with groanings which cannot be expressed in speech. He who searches hearts knows what the Spirit means, for the Spirit intercedes for the saints as God himself wills" (Romans 8:26-27). It is a divine irony that real prayer is God conversing with himself. It is a saving grace that, if we choose to let him, he will carry on this sublime exchange within us and for us.

> Each night the waiting women met
> to wake the heavens with their plea
> that God almighty not forget
> their sons upon the stormy sea.
>
> One misty dawn five ships returned
> to tempered welcome tinged with pain
> for Fearless lightning-struck and burned
> now lay still manned beneath the main.
>
> Did he who heard the mothers call
> find fault with some who spoke his name
> or might the One who fashioned all
> at times distracted lose the game?

Maker of heaven and earth, giver of each breath, hope of all who sail upon the sea of life, I open myself to the movement of the Spirit working within me. In communion with your obedient Son, I seek to make your will my own. Guide my going each day and give me safe haven at journey's end. Amen.

FIFTH SUNDAY OF EASTER

I heard a loud voice from the throne cry out: "This is God's dwelling among men. He shall dwell with them and they shall be his people and he shall be their God who is always with them. He shall wipe away every tear from their eyes, and there shall be no more death or mourning, crying out or pain, for the former world has passed away."

The One who sat on the throne said to me, "See, I make all things new!" (Revelation 21:3-5).

Against the burnished gold of the tabernacle dances the lively flame. Across the nave, the great doors open to admit a weary visitor and an invigorating gust of spring air. In welcome, the flame becomes more vibrant, more urgent, beckoning the seeker to come closer, to enter the charmed circle of those who skip and leap in the unseen radiance of which the flickering lamp is but a feeble testimony.

How many to their loss have forgotten the music of meditation in the Real Presence? How many more have never known this sacred song? The contending voices of contemporary life afflict even the most well-intentioned, drawing them away from the rhythmic serenity of self-release found in the selfless adoration of the incarnation of divine love. Perhaps the reformed liturgy has made God too accessible, too much the paterfamilias presiding with breezy informality over his presumptuous children. Even respect for the mystery of the Godhead can be diluted by overly-familiar presiders, insipid hymnody bland enough to be acceptable to any denomination, and congregations clad in jeans and jogging shoes. If Masses must be smarmy enough to make absolutely everyone comfortable, then there should be a place, an ambience for the expression of unrestrained awe in the presence of omnipotence.

There is. Entering the circle of light cast by the tabernacle lamp, one inhales the timeless perfume which sustained Adam and Eve in their ballet of innocence. To say only that the flickering flame is a reassuring sign of the reservation of the Blessed Sacrament is not to say enough. Behind the golden door lie the focus of God's mercy on humankind and the locus of divine dynamism in the midst of his lethargic people. It is not possible for the recollected visitor to abide long in this place before he or she slips time's moorings to recall the history of sacrifice which led to the institution of the Eucharist and the guidance of the Spirit over the subsequent twenty centuries which has guaranteed the Real Presence to this day.

Participation in the modern Mass means bringing God into the now. Indeed, many liturgists pride themselves on using found objects and current events to pierce the veil of mystery in which the deity has always been shrouded. Prayer before the tabernacle, however, seeks the reverse, a passage from priority and deadline into mystery and eternity. This is a difficult adjustment for most contemporary Christians bound as they are so securely to the moment. An authentic act of the will is required, a deliberate disengagement from the embrace of high-tech and instant communication. To seek the Lord of heaven and earth is to stand naked and alone before the smoking mountain, to be rid of protective busyness, even to evade the worthy petitions of the needy and friendless. This is a time for creature to become accessible to Creator.

Find your place before the tabernacle today, and there let the flickering lamp be a sign of the dance of God behind the golden door. Allow yourself to be enticed by the movement of love and mercy within the Holy of Holies. In disentangling your soul from the coils of time and necessity, you will be drawn into the eternal music. All this will come slowly, however, for as with most, your schedule, your projects, even your worries can be part of a comfortable cloak against the untested revelation of God's love. Although you may revel in modernity, you are afraid of what is really new. Let God circle you in the halo of love radiating from the tabernacle. Let him untie the knots of weariness and concern which bind you to the world. He seeks to free you for the dance of King David, to have you leap before the Ark of the New Covenant and skip away from time's dirge, away from the protestations of a world wanting always to lead. For now, be still, and let the Holy One speak his invitation to the dance: "See, I make all things new."

> a secret shouted to the skies
> a love provoking hate
> a cornerstone to trip the wise
> a much too narrow gate
> a truth condemned by purchased lies
> a pawn to tame the great
> a silence stirring coarse replies
> a man against a state
> a priest without Levitic ties
> a king in thrall to fate
> a tomb from which new life did rise
> a cross to venerate
> a prisoned God before my eyes
> a host to contemplate
> a list of riddles that defies
> a glib sophisticate

All-powerful God, you have hidden your might in our midst so that we may approach your majesty without fear. Encircle us with the mystery of divine love. Enlighten us with your eternal truth. Open our eyes to a new day, a new way. Amen.

MONDAY OF THE FIFTH WEEK

> Jesus said to his disciples:
> "This much have I told you
> while I was still with you;
> the Paraclete, the Holy Spirit
> whom the Father will send in my name,
> will instruct you in everything,
> and remind you all that I told you"
> (John 14:25-26).

He was awakened by a cow lowing very near the window. A cow didn't seem right somehow. Nor did the venetian blinds slicing the morning sun. As he groped for the bathroom door, the puzzle grew geometrically, assuming the shape of a black hole, a pulsing crater filled with nothing smack in the middle of his memory. Through the blinds in the bathroom he saw a pasture. There was the cow rubbing her neck on a fence post. He rapped on the glass to get her attention; perhaps the animal would verify his existence. She ignored him.

No wallet, no suitcase, only the clothes he had slept in. And no name! It wasn't even on the tip of his tongue. It was in the black hole. Fear hobbled him as he eased into the hallway. Maybe he had been robbed. At the head of the stairs, he looked down on two uniformed men lounging at a desk. They turned to watch his careful descent. He was ashamed of his rumpled clothes, more ashamed to ask if this was a jail. "No, pal," said the one behind the desk. "The jail's on the other side. You are the guest of Sheriff Delton Miles, friend of the downtrodden." The officer smirked. "He put you up in his spare room 'cause you looked 'responsible.' " The other snickered. "Siddown. Have a cup."

He told them he couldn't even remember his name, much less where he came from or how he got here. Where was here? "Copeland County Sheriff's Office, Madison, Wyoming. A trucker dropped you off last night. Said you were sick or something. The Sheriff couldn't find any identification on you, so you're going to Casper on the one-thirty bus." Wyoming. Was that good or bad? Was he close to home? Did he have a home? Did he have someone? "Casper's the V A Hospital. Sheriff thinks you're a vet." Why a vet? "I dunno. Says you just look like a vet." He put the coffee down, covered his eyes, and wept for a loss beyond measure, for a life beyond knowing.

So that you and I wouldn't have to wake up every morning and reinvent our Christian lives, Jesus promised his Holy Spirit to remind us "of all that I told you." It is the Spirit which moves us to our prayers, the Spirit which guides our relationships with others, the Spirit which gives us hope when things look bleak. Our past is part of the history of the Church, a community of believers governed by the Spirit for two thousand years. Our future is the eternal banquet to which the Spirit invites us each day and for which the Spirit prepares us in the sacraments. It is not necessary to start each day with a *tabula rasa*, a clean slate, for the Holy Spirit reminds us of who we are and where we are going.

What if it were otherwise? Suppose you woke up tomorrow morning a spiritual amnesiac. Consider your path through a day without the guidance of the Holy Spirit. You can't offer your favorite prayer. You have no prayers. At work, what keeps you from joining in the malicious gossip? You have no conscience. When the whistle blows, a few drinks at the bar. More than a few; you only live once. You have no other prospects. Home to a family that must be made to obey your every whim. After all, they are accidents of atoms and your world spins around Number One. Then off to bed without dreams of the past or hope for the future. No one has made you any promises.

In your meditation today, fill in the personal details of twenty-four hours in the absence of the Holy Spirit. You will come quickly to feel like a fish upon the shore, bereft of nourishment and direction, your only hope that the tide will roll back in time to save you for one more empty day. Then give thanks to the loving Lord for a yesterday spanning twenty centuries and a tomorrow which can last forever, all yours in the embrace of his Spirit.

> Remember the Garden
> before the flaming sword
> when you and Eve and Adam all
> went walking with the Lord?
>
> Remember the groaning
> as earth and sea and sky
> in mighty separation formed
> beneath the Planner's eye?
>
> Remember when nothing
> existed save for space
> in which the Holy Persons were
> soft-locked in love's embrace?
>
> Remember, O Christian,
> in Spirit you were there,
> a gleam within the Father's eye;
> your flesh the Son would share.

Holy Spirit, recall for us our beginnings in the mind of the Creator. Guide us each day in the footsteps of our Savior. Hold before our eyes the heritage of heaven. Accept this prayer of gratitude for holy lineage, divine sustenance, and promised glory.   Amen.

TUESDAY OF THE FIFTH WEEK

> Jesus said to his disciples:
> " 'Peace' is my farewell to you,
> my peace is my gift to you;
> I do not give it to you
>   as the world gives peace"   (John 14:27).

"Have a nice day." In striped pinafore, she was as pert as any counter girl on television. From beneath her jaunty cap streamed the scrubbed and saucy optimism which Americans want when they buy hamburgers. Hadn't he seen her on a poster lately with that new breakfast combination? Then she was gone, blessing another customer with hip innocence. He shuffled to the cash register, a sleepwalker roused by a too-bright star, afraid to look at the cashier counting out his change, afraid of more straw-blond hair and snapping blue eyes and accusing perkiness. He couldn't stop his ears, though. "Have a nice day."

Remember the last time you heard it? Perhaps it was at the bank this morning after the teller handed over the final fifty in your account. Or maybe yesterday at the drugstore when the clerk slipped your laxative into a see-through plastic bag. It isn't until you really need a nice day that you become aware that the world is powerless to bless. No matter how hopeful the words, they are just that. They cannot lighten your laundry load, reduce your mortgage, or cure your arthritis.

Jesus' words are of a different order. His blessing of peace brings palpable serenity, soothing balm for the seething soul, if you can meet one condition, if you will admit that the peace of Christ has nothing to do with masking the reality of neuritis or neuralgia or unsightly wax build-up. Unlike Burger Betty, he is not merely hoping that good news might be yours, nor does he promise a rearrangement of your day to remove the slings and arrows. He is the repository, the proprietor of peace, and he gives what is his own.

The disciples, who thought that Jesus' farewell meant protection from poverty and hostility and pain, were rudely disabused of any such notion early on in their mission. They found, instead, that to protect them against irrational fate, he had given them the example of filial piety, trusting obedience to the Father's will which is the peace that passes understanding. As long as they remained faithful to his way, they would possess sure hope, not that of miraculous rescue from trial, but the confidence born of doing God's will. To bolster their resolve, in bestowing his peace upon the disciples, the Prince of Peace gave them himself, the perfect embodiment of trust in God.

Interior peace is the fruit of this trust. The soul can have a nice day no matter what the body suffers, no matter how confused the mind. The serenity of St. Ignatius of Antioch on his journey to death in Rome is a good example of the peace which Christ brings to those who accept his gift of self. Indeed, Ignatius' only anxiety was that his friends in Rome might somehow block the legal process. "I will gladly die for God if only you do not stand in my way. I plead with you: show me no untimely kindness. Let me be food for the wild beasts, for they are my way to God" (A Letter to the Romans). He opened himself to a higher wisdom and trusted not in rescue but in the love of God. He was confident that with Christ dwelling in him he could only do the Father's work. Ignatius and all martyrs teach us that the secret of inner peace is conformity to and trust in God's will.

Plan to have a nice day today. You deserve it. Do not be anxious about the barriers to happiness or accomplishment which are sure to arise. By now, you should have grasped life's bittersweet lesson: No matter how well-made your plans, human frailty and accidents of nature will have their way. They may shake you like a rag doll, but they cannot disturb the peace of Christ resting in your heart. There, in the inner depths, is the still-point in the midst of chaos. There is the day the Lord has made for you. There, you will match your shaky step to his serene stride, doing the Father's will, sharing the Son's trust.

centripetal	centrifugal
the force of woe	the whirl of joy
collapsing star	exploding star
collecting care	expanding love
compressing fear	exposing trust
upon a heart	within a heart
bituminous	coterminous
beneath despair's	with Jesus' own
ill-fated weight	still-point of peace
a life is crushed	a life is freed

Lord Jesus, in the midst of my worries and disappointments, let me not forget your calm obedience to the Father's will. Through betrayal, torture, and even death, you honored him with your confident hope. Your trusting heart is the peaceful center of the universe. Make my heart like unto Thine.   Amen.

WEDNESDAY OF THE FIFTH WEEK

> Jesus said:
> "I am the true vine
> and my Father is the vinegrower.
> He prunes away
> every barren branch,
> but the fruitful ones
> he trims clean
> to increase their yield"   (John 15:1-2).

Slim stalks of sugar cane lie huddled against the advancing fire. They will not, can not resist the purifying flame, for the flashing knife has done its work. With one sharp stroke the stream of life is severed, distended roots relax with sudden release from their search. On a deathbed of its own leaves, the cane settles stiffly, waiting, as sweet smoke blurs the line between earth and heaven.

Field fires are set by sugar men at harvest time to speed the process. Once, the stalks were trimmed by many hands before the cane was crushed; now, controlled fires tended by a few workers prune ten acres in a day and a night. The flames are not allowed to linger lest they ravage the tender stalks; the fire feeds only upon the barren bed of leaves, moving quickly, a veil of purgation swept along by merciful hands. Soon, on a soft autumn morning, the haze of smoke and river fog will be parted by the advance of the big-wheeled carts carrying blackened poles of *Saccharum officinarum* to the grinding mill.

Whether it will last an instant or an eon, only the Father knows, but each of us will see the cleansing flame in its inexorable progress. The flashing blade will topple the tall and vibrant, release the sickly and aged; all will lie upon life's last horizon, supine, defenseless against the fire of truth. Too late regret, too late reform on Purgatory's smoking plain. The leaves in which we hid ourselves — the lies, the petty jealousies, the base motives — will curl and craze in the heat of divine candor. Where once we stood ramrod straight in the green finery of pride, then we shall pull at our sins to strip them away as self-recognition sears our souls. We will not succeed, for the knife has fallen and the Just One must do what we would not.

To think upon the last things is salutary. If we will not reform our lives out of love for God, perhaps we shall do so out of love for self. Do not be misled by those who would paint Purgatory as merely a temporary state of waiting until the soul is ready to gaze upon the face of God. Purgatory is not an anteroom of heaven where the slightly-chagrined count the tiles in the floor until their numbers are called. A personal history of sin, a life incompatible with Christ's teaching demands more than simple embarrassment. Leaves of pride grown tall obstruct the soul's vision; they must be consumed by truth, if not in this life, then hereafter. Folly has its price. Thanks to God's mercy, at least part of that price can be paid before the harvest.

As you meditate this day on your final day, let not concern become panic. A better life can begin now. You can renew your commitment to God's law now. You can forestall a later purgation by making amends now. Repair the damage. Seek reconciliation. Let the reforming flame touch you today. There will be pain in the measure in which you caused pain, but remember the cane and its ultimate destination, a fate infinitely more horrible than transient fire. Through the compassion of God, not all must be thrown between the grinding wheels. In sugar country, children stand along the road to the mill, eager to snatch a blackened stalk from the high carts. Sometimes they succeed, and joyfully sip the sweet nectar refined in the fire. God sends just such angels to rescue you and me.

> Test not God's patience, my fickle friend.
> One day His mercy will have an end.
> The choice is glory or timeless woe.
> *Memento mori* before you go.

Just Father, in my sinfulness, I have presumed upon your mercy. Purify my foolish heart here and now. Let the crucible of life prepare me to share the sweet victory of the saints.   Amen.

THURSDAY OF THE FIFTH WEEK

Peter said to the apostles and the elders:
   "God, who reads the hearts of men, showed his approval by granting the Holy Spirit to them just as he did to us. He made no distinction between them and us, but purified their hearts by means of faith also. Why, then, do you put God to the test by trying to place on the shoulders of these converts a yoke which neither we nor our fathers were able to bear?"
   (Acts 15:8-10).

The candidate deserves our votes because she has paid her dues in the long election process. The boxer has earned a shot at the title by paying his dues in a hundred prelims. Because she paid her dues in a lifetime of smoky lounges, the torch singer claims top billing. The term arose in the days when labor unions were beginning to flex their muscles. Poor men and women, not always able to pay their union dues with cash, were considered for leadership if they had paid the price on perilous picket lines and in contentious organizing campaigns. Local officials who came up through the ranks were trusted for their experience in the trenches rather than for their degrees or pedigrees.

In every group endeavor this test of acceptability has the advantage of simplicity. A single question is the litmus: Does she or he share our history of striving and suffering? Intelligence, efficiency, education are secondary; analysis of such is subject to the vagaries of human perception and prejudice. Not so when it comes to the payment of dues. Did he stand with us? Was she baptized in the common struggle?

The earliest Christians saw the passion, death, and Resurrection of Christ as the culmination of historic struggles stretching back to the testing of Abraham. Waiting for the Messiah meant enduring holy wars, exile, slavery, and foreign domination. After the Resurrection, the followers of the Way were *illuminati* in the midst of their blind brothers and sisters; their first impulse was to enlighten the seed of Abraham, to make clear to the circumcised that the long preparation was over. Then Peter brought to Jerusalem news that pagans had received the Holy Spirit. It was very hard to swallow. After all, the Gentiles had not paid their dues. If these outsiders had not starved in the Desert of Sin, if they had not languished in Babylon or wept over the Abomination of Desolation, at least they could make a reverence to all the Jews had suffered. Was it too much to ask for a ritual shedding of blood?

Peter informed the first council of the Church that it was, indeed, too much. His dream of the canvas lowered from heaven with the birds and the beasts, the command to slaughter and eat clean and unclean alike revealed a powerful mandate for the universalization of the Good News. The pouring out of the Spirit upon the household of the Roman,

Cornelius, confirmed Peter's vision. It seemed that a history of striving, a thousand years of longing could be compressed into an act of faith. The apostles and elders decided that, when it came to conversion, accounts payable could be an interior summing up, that the circumcision which mattered was one of a heart cleansed in the blood of Christ. As St. Paul wrote to the converts from paganism at Colossae, "You were also circumcised in him, not with the circumcision administered by hand but with Christ's circumcision which strips off the carnal body completely" (Colossians 2:11). The workers hired last were to receive the same wage as those who labored all day long in the heat of the sun. It was hard to swallow then; it is hard to swallow now.

Check your attitude toward those who appear not to have paid their dues. Look at the excluded and the marginalized, those yearning to enjoy the perquisites of the great middle class. Whom do you see? Recent immigrants who did not sweat to build this country. Welfare mothers avoiding traditional sacrifices on behalf of their children. The homeless who would not save a little each month for a down payment on a house. Young black men refusing to do menial work and waiting for a handout. Native Americans awash in alcohol.

Now lift over their heads the lamp of life renewed. Let its beam of truth dispel the stereotypes which you have allowed to shape your thinking. Just as the pagans seemed alien to Peter until he sat down to eat with them, so will those you've painted with such a broad brush until you see them with Christ's eyes. Up close, each of them looks like a child of God, the God who sent his Son to those who seemed not to have paid their dues — the tax collector, the prostitute, and, yes, the Gentile. That startlingly new idea of universal mission which Peter brought to the Council of Jerusalem was a call to disregard the ancient account book, to cross the borders of Israel, to breach the walls of tradition, to break out of the self-imprisonment of stereotype, to give living witness to Christ's teaching that God's love is neither deserved nor earned, but pure gift offered to all.

End today's meditation by allowing the radiance of the Resurrection to fall upon your own soul. How much of this country did you sweat to build? How long have you been jobless? Have you never received a helping hand at a critical moment in your life? "Why, then, do you put God to the test by trying to place on the shoulders of these converts a yoke which neither we nor our fathers were able to bear?" There are dues and there are dues, but no one is able to buy the Good News. No one needs to.

> The favored few
>   content to rest in certainty
>   that God has blessed their fortunes
>   over those who yearn for dignity
>   will someday learn a lesson clear
>   of Love's descent upon the earth
>   to pitch his tent among the poorest
>   there to speak of glory
>   to the mild and meek.

God of the nations, make each of us a missionary in our own little world. Protect us from the fear of reaching out to strangers. Let us recognize what you see in them: the dignity of your creation. We are all your children, thanking you for our beginnings, trusting you with our endings. Amen.

FRIDAY OF THE FIFTH WEEK

> My heart is steadfast, O god;
> > my heart is steadfast;
> I will sing and chant praise.
> Awake, O my soul; awake
> > lyre and harp!
> I will wake the dawn!
> I will give thanks to you among the
> > peoples, O Lord,
> I will chant your praise
> > among the nations (Psalm 57:8-10).

At first, a Thursday night visitor to the choir loft might be edified at the courtesy shown to the unpunctual Herm Hoffman. The tenors would shift their ranks to provide the space toward which he stubbornly headed. The sopranos would edge closer to the Director. A more perceptive onlooker might note the widening gap on the third riser, the continuing movement of the whole choir away from the invisible "X" that marked Herm's spot. It was the Big Bang theory in sharps and flats. As usual, he wasn't just late; they had already practiced for an hour. Nor was the cause of his delay undetectable; his breath made the altos' eyes water as he bulled his way past averted heads.

After four years of such indelicate entrances, the gentlemen and ladies of Emmanuel Lutheran's adult choir had given up hope of rescue. The last to surrender was Director Theiler who told concerned members a year ago Christmas that he would not lead another delegation to the Parsonage. Reverend Uberburg's song was always the same. Herm had come a long way from the drunk tank. Herm needs to be accepted. Herm would probably not be in church if he weren't with the choir. But most of all — and here every protesting group started as the Pastor's clenched fist came down upon his spindly desk — Herman Hoffman could sing! Even in his cups, he could sing circles around anyone in town! That was the signal for Mrs. Uberburg to bring out the cookies. She knew that the Pastor's desk and the tenor section were both weak. Before her husband began his rehabilitation program, stifled guffaws were heard on Sunday mornings when the choir attempted to soar to merely sub-angelic heights. Sober on the Lord's Day, Herm with his range and control added a good twenty songs to the repertoire, making it the envy of every minister in the central part of the state. Even after stumbling up the steps of the loft to interrupt the weekly practice, he would carry the choir away from the bemused Mr. Theiler, seeing and grasping harmonic opportunities only a professional would chance. And in most cases, he was gloriously, triumphantly correct.

So, every Thursday night, and Tuesday too before Christmas and Easter, three dozen of the staunchest of German Lutherans resigned themselvess to meeting and working with a tenor well past tipsy. Self-preservation was one motive; there would hardly be a choir without him. Prestige played a part; they accepted many invitations from other churches on off-Sundays. With the passing of time and after repeated homilies in the Parsonage, some members came to see a weightier argument against Herm's banishment. The Emmanuel Choir could praise God as no other. Their "Mighty Fortress" no longer poured a flood of mortal ills upon the congregation nor conjured the face of the Prince of darkness, but now told the Truth which triumphs and revealed the name of the Lord Sabaoth. The dream of the Scourge of Wittenberg became flesh and blood every other Sunday at 10:00 a.m. They filled the church with the power of God, a power surging from thirty-six steadfast hearts and one parched throat.

In our neo-pagan world, no Christian of any denomination may enjoy the luxury of self-righteousness. Our numbers are too small to permit the presumption that our mission is to separate the darnel from the good seed. From the unborn to the elderly, God uses the weak to confound the strong. On the cross, ultimate weakness became the instrument of ultimate power. How many of those in the congregation at Emmanuel Lutheran were lifted up to the face of God by one man? How many in the choir loft were moved to admit their own failings? As for the troubled tenor himself, could any believer be bold enough to deny that, when it comes to God's desire to save, the singer is sung by the song?

> Mockingbirds and hooting owls warted frogs and crows
> gathered round a forest pool as the sun arose.
> Croaking toad and crooning loon whippoorwill and jay
> each poured forth a hymn of thanks for the newborn day.
>
> Distant hunters heard and winced at the raucous song
> while the great Conductor smiled and just hummed along.
> Was it noisy discord or music of the blest?
> Patient is the Lord's baton till the final rest.

Father-Creator, all the world is your handiwork. Each of your creatures bears the mark of your loving purpose. Give us the tolerance and the sensitivity to confirm your design in the least of our brothers and sisters.   Amen.

SATURDAY OF THE FIFTH WEEK

> Jesus said to his disciples:
> "Remember what I told you:
> no slave is greater than his master.
> They will harry you
> as they harried me.
> They will respect your words
> as much as they respected mine"   (John 15:20).

Most Christians in Western society know little of overt religious persecution. Except for that of immigrants from totalitarian regimes, experience of state-sponsored discrimination is second hand. Russia's all-pervasive atheism, Idi Amin's bloody Uganda, the keening streets of Northern Ireland come to mind but rarely, usually at the behest of an aloof anchorman. The protection of enlightened national charters permits the satisfaction of armchair outrage over the hounding of innocents in faraway lands. To this sophisticated century, the words of Jesus in John's Gospel seem not to apply. The question for today is: Should they?

Should the public witness of faith cause more trouble than it does? A nation which combines authentic religious freedom with a high standard of living produces little in the way of harassment. Collaboration is the key to assimilation; zeal is for the few who take a perverse pleasure in standing outside the pale. Rocking the boat will get you thrown overboard. Yet, the words haunt us. If we have not been harried, if we have never been scorned for swimming against the tide of secular society, perhaps the triumph of the cross will not be ours. The question has even found its way to a famous "Wanted" poster. Above the outline of a featureless face are listed the crimes: commitment, charity, devotion, altruism, courage, outspokenness. And below: If you were hailed into court on charges of being a Christian, would there be enough evidence to convict you?

The first step in changing from a comfortable Christian to a convicted Christian would be an examination of conscience based on a more contemporary Decalogue. The ten laws listed here are completely arbitrary and altogether tendentious. Each convert from ease to zeal is free to add his or her own counts to this indictment of apathy:

1. Thou shalt not pass the pornographic magazines behind the cashier's counter without asking for the manager and lodging a complaint.
2. Thou shalt not gather again in the lunch room unless the backstabbers are informed of the harm they do.
3. Thou shalt not condone a teenager's drug use or sexual adventurism because everybody else does it.
4. Thou shalt not leave the whistle unblown when fellow workers steal from the factory.
5. Thou shalt not give in to a spouse's demand for unnatural sexual practices.
6. Thou shalt not smile in approving silence while the rest of the gang defaces public property.
7. Thou shalt not be afraid to chastise a friend for driving under the influence.
8. Thou shalt not have more important things to do when asked to join in picketing an abortion clinic.
9. Thou shalt not participate in creative bookkeeping when the business needs just one little break at tax time.
10. Thou shalt not preach a homily on the joys of heaven when racial tensions are destroying the local schools.

Obedience to any one of these new commandments can generate a heap of trouble with friends, co-workers, schoolmates, or family members. Remember, Jesus did not dissemble when it came to the challenge of discipleship. "Father will be split against son and son against father, mother against daughter and daughter against mother" (Luke 12:52). "You will be delivered up even by your parents, brothers, relatives, and friends" (Luke 21:16). When the practice of faith becomes indistinguishable from membership in a cozy social club, then the practitioners lose the ability to offer God the highest praise, that is, sacrifice. The worldly-wise tell us no one goes looking for trouble. Jesus seems to say just the opposite. He came to this world because there was trouble here. There still is. What price will you and I pay to do something about it?

> A hundred thousand tiny bytes
> make one computer's meal,
> four thousand r. p. m.'s will spin
> the station wagon's wheel.
>
> Ten flashing clocks steal now from then
> as breathless we submit
> to schedulequotadeadline tight
> as life and limb permit.
>
> A hundred sixty-eight less one
> upon the seventh day,
> a hundred sixty-seven done
> before we kneel to pray.
>
> One hour of peace with twenty-three
> devoted to the whirl
> of shoppingsweepingfootball leaves
> this solitary pearl.

No wonder folks who come to church
complain of hearts awry,
resigned to nothing better than
a sixty minute sigh.

Eternal Lord, zeal without patience is sound and fury signifying nothing. In the frenzied rush of time, slow us down enough to make each moment sacred. Tomorrow we leave to you; your will be done in us today. Amen.

SIXTH SUNDAY OF EASTER

Jesus said to his disciples:
"If you love me
and obey the command I give you,
I will ask the Father
and he will give you another Paraclete —
to be with you always:
the Spirit of truth,
whom the world cannot accept,
since it neither sees him nor recognizes him;
but you can recognize him
because he remains with you
and will be within you"   (John 14:15-17).

A piercing light is truth. Its steely beam illuminates broad vistas and hidden corners alike. What is good and holy sparkles in the radiance; what is crass and unworthy shines like a dead fish on the shore. Truth is impartial and unblinking. Sometimes called the cold truth, it can seem merciless on the lips of a doctor reporting the results of a biopsy.

Truth hurts. Not many pilgrims go out of their way to seek it, but they would be lost without its constant guidance. Acceptance of truth often depends on who conveys it. Since the light of truth is absolutely necessary for Christian life, great responsibility falls upon those who bear the lamp.

Jesus Christ bore the lamp of truth. In his lifetime, few accepted it. He was merciful and forgiving, plain-spoken and courageous, the perfect truth-teller. They hung him on a cross. Truth hurts not just the hearer. His followers were fearful, ambitious, short-sighted, as weak as any other human being. If they were to live long enough to tell the truth, if the world was to listen long enough to accept their message, something supernatural had to happen. Even the lamp glowing with the truth of Christ's risen life would sputter and die when the oxygen of tolerance in Jerusalem was used up. The light for the whole world needed more air, the lamp-bearer needed longer legs.

Jesus called the Holy Spirit *another* Paraclete. He himself had been the first, guiding the disciples on their journeys within Israel, accusing the Sadducees and Pharisees of hypocrisy, chiding common folks for their stubbornness, revealing the kingdom to the poor. His light would be put out. As reported in John's Gospel, Jesus' farewell address included the promise of another lamp-bearer to stiffen the spines of the disciples, to open the eyes of those blind to the truth, to make the world wonder about the glow in the East. As Jesus had illumined the path of his followers for three years, now the new Paraclete would guide his Church to the end of time.

Advocate. Intercessor. Counselor. Protector. Support. To the extent that we welcome the Holy Spirit into our lives and share with others some part of his message of truth, we bear the lamp with and accept the many titles of the Paraclete. The Spirit's guidance of the Church extends from hierarchs to hoi polloi; for most of us, the task is to keep one candle glowing in the private darkness of a brother or sister. The truth can hurt, but it can heal as well. As advocates, we stand beside the poor man who pleads his case before the welfare examiner. We vouch for the truth of his plight. As intercessors, we spend time on our knees in petition for the girl attempting to break a drug habit. We confirm the truth of her good intentions. As counselors, we advise the youth wondering about a religious vocation. We affirm the truth of his searching. As protectors, we shield an elderly couple from unscrupulous insurance agents. We champion the truth of their dignity. As supporters, we encourage the honest neighbor to enter the School Board race. We underwrite the truth of her zeal. In all this, we give the lamp-bearer longer legs. We act as agents of the Paraclete in building up the body of Christ.

In cooperating with the Paraclete, we must be as gentle as Jesus when he meant the truth to heal, and as forthright as Jesus when he knew the truth would be rejected. There are many ways to tell the truth, but there is no alternative to the truth. And, lest this delicate balance between healing and convicting intimidate us to the point of fearful silence, we should remember that no one who bears the lamp with the Paraclete can predict the outcome. Although Jesus was gentle with the young man who kept the commandments, the truth was too hard to take when it came to giving up material possessions. On the other hand, despite the resistance of most Jewish leaders to Jesus' vehement charges of hypocrisy, some, like Nicodemus, came secretly to him. The servants of the Paraclete are incapable of knowing the final result of their cooperation. We must tell the truth and rely for its effectiveness on its divine source.

Today, think of your role as lamp-bearer in building up the body of Christ. No matter what your vocation, no matter how insignificant a part you may think you play, by your Baptism and Confirmation, you have been sent to strengthen the Church with the truth. There can be no more important work than healing the Christian community's wounds and witnessing to its glory. Hold the lamp high and trust in the Paraclete. If conveyed with a balance of delicacy and conviction, the truth will light the way for the Church and its members, errant and sure-footed alike, bound for the kingdom. Hold the lamp high and trust in the Paraclete.

> Galileo Galilei
> came to Rome upon a donkey.
> Veritas, his mount was named.
> Lies, the Inquisition claimed.
>
> Stood the man on parquet flooring,
> just outside the beast was snoring.
> Earth is not a whirling mass,
> said the priests, don't be an ass.
>
> Wakened, Truth commenced to braying,
> shook the windows with her neighing,
> drowning out the judge's call
> to recant, to gainsay all.
>
> In the dock, he kept repeating
> what his tethered friend was beating
> on the stones with angry hooves:
> Nonetheless, my dears, it moves.

Bright Spirit of Truth, we often shrink from bringing your message to a world grown comfortable with lies. Strengthen our resolve to carry high your purifying light. In times of doubt, remind us that the messenger is cleansed by the message, the lamp-bearer ennobled by the flames. Amen.

MONDAY OF THE SIXTH WEEK

> We put out to sea from Troas and set a course straight for Samothrace, and the next day on to Neapolis; from there we went to Philippi, a leading city in the district of Macedonia and a Roman colony. We spent some time in that city (Acts 16:11-12).

Memory is a map stretching back into the haze of auld lang syne. While the places we visited last month are alive with detail, those in the distance lose definition. As we grow older, vast deserts appear on the map of memory. We skipped or slogged across them once, but now they seem to be trackless wastes. If, as it must, life still teems in these forgotten regions, we know it not.

In the latter chapters of the Acts of the Apostles, Luke attempts to stave off forgetfulness by reminding the young Christian community of Paul's heroic journeys. In places like Philippi and Athens, the Apostle to the Gentiles made an indelible mark. Details of his debates, conversions, imprisonments, and escapes make for vivid reading, but there are many other cities and districts which get barely a mention. What did it profit a primitive Christian to know that Paul went to Derbe or Lystra, through Phrygia and Mysia? Why should a frightened follower of a Way now suspect throughout the Roman Empire care that Attalia, Neapolis, and Samothrace were on the preacher's itinerary?

The Acts of the Apostles could be called a map of remembrance written for one Theophilus. In dedicating this work and his Gospel to a friend of God, Luke meant to enhance the collective memory of the Christian community. Among his aims was the preservation of proof that Jesus' command was being carried out, that is, the mandate to preach penance for the remission of sins to *all* nations. In the lore of the early Church, Derbe and Neapolis were important, for the world lived there as much as in Athens and Rome. There was to be no desert of forgetfulness surrounding the capitals of power. The meek as well as the great were to be offered salvation. The name, Theophilus, itself may have been a literary convention, a Greek word standing for the Gentile world, for all nations awaiting the Good News.

All friends of God needed then and need now to be reminded that the essential and, therefore, the most important events in the work of renewing the face of the earth take place in human hearts. As there were hearts yearning in Mitylene in 58 A.D., so was your heart longing for a healing word that unremarkable day nearly hidden in the mists of your personal history.

Today, exercise your Christian memory. Push back the haze of years, not to high profile occasions such as First Communion or Confirmation, but to the Derbes and Lystras of your spiritual life. Don't let the pageantry or anxiety surrounding a Wedding or an Ordination rivet your attention. Go into the desert and retrace the barely discernible path. Here is that hour alone in a hushed church when God's will became clear to you. There is that cold day when the poor child appeared at the door. And over there, the time of private sorrow you had to bear alone until Jesus put his hand on your shoulder. He waited in that out-of-the-way place because he knew you needed him.

Rest beside the road from Derbe to Lystra. The gift of memory allows you to see what was then the future. How far you've come. How momentous was that which seemed so insignificant at the time. God whispered and rescued you on one commonplace day. He whispers still, off the beaten track, away from the hurly-burly. He speaks his healing word in the hearts of anonymous Christians. In tones most ordinary, he tells of love extraordinary. Awesome events may turn a million heads, but the world is saved in murmurs. You remember, don't you, when God whispered and saved you for today?

> From grandiose basilica to famed cathedral fled
> an anxious pilgrim shadowed by the news that God was dead.
> Illuminating words he sought in murky gothic naves,
> yet spurned the roadside chapel with its neon "Jesus Saves"
> which washed the threadbare congregants in intermittent light,
> a humble beacon bold enough to check the endless night.

Humble Savior, you did not deem equality with God something to be grasped at. You emptied yourself and took the form of a slave. In this season of glory and joy, let me not forget that there would be no triumph to celebrate without the poverty of the cross. Amen.

TUESDAY OF THE SIXTH WEEK

> Jesus said to his disciples:
> "Now that I go back to him who sent me,
>   not one of you asks me,
>   'Where are you going?'
> Because I have had all this to say to you,
>   you are overcome with grief" (John 16:5-6).

Now they knew the worst. The light of their lives would be put out, leaving them sightless sheep in the midst of wolves. Each time he had said it before in simile and allusion there seemed to be two ways to take the words. Harried slaves still get fed. A trimmed branch will bud again. But in the last few moments, his features had darkened. There was a line between his eyes they had not seen since that day he approached the tomb of Lazarus. Despite the closed windows, the candles began to gutter as a chill breath swept the room. Not only would they be expelled from synagogues, their deaths would prove the piety of their executioners. Their deaths! They always believed they would come to no harm in the presence of their protector. The only way the authorities could get to them was if.... Even as he chided them for their lack of attention to his fate they were blinded by despair over their own.

The pain of loss is a wintry mixture of loneliness, regret, self-pity, and insult. The one who has gone leaves a hole in your life. You keep falling into the space which she once occupied. You catch yourself whispering to thin air. The rhythm of the day is interrupted again and again because you can no longer share little jokes and angers with her. You may not be alone, but you are no longer complete. Your life has begun to disintegrate, leaving you unsure that the process can be stopped.

At odd times, the memory of his need brings you up short. You wonder whether you did enough for him while he was here. The List forms in your mind: I was ungenerous on November 14th, self-absorbed on the 23rd, insensitive December 2nd. Perhaps a more considerate witness to his worth would have caused him to delay, even cancel, his departure plans.

Could anyone expect you to survive the absence of her smile, her loving touch? No one should be surprised to see you in this state of collapse. Their consolation is well-deserved; you let them know, however, that it is quite ineffectual. No one could possibly understand your loss. They didn't know the depth of your love. You must teach them with your tears.

The unfeeling hand of fate or God or the European Subsidiaries Manager has swept him off the map of your life. The powers-that-be thought too little of your rights. It must be so obvious that you are someone who can be pushed around. What a mistaken judgment of your value! Now you are driven to suffer fools and loss alike.

Loneliness. Regret. Self-pity. Insult. Surely these specters hung heavily in the Upper Room. They formed a murky curtain around the Apostles, insulating them from all the words of hope spoken that evening, dulling their concern for the Master and his destination. Numbed by grief over their own prospects, twelve picked men turned inward, away from the promise of the Paraclete, away from the pledges they had made with such alacrity at seashore and city gate, away from the chance to live on.

Look beyond loss today. A dear one may have died. A good friend moves away. You missed the promotion by a hair. The new school is nothing like the old. You can't help feeling alone, sorry you didn't do more. Licking your wounds has its comforts. And the supervisor who passed you over . . . well, yes, he is a jerk. These are all natural feelings, but hardly make a life's work. Sooner rather than later in your grieving process, you must lay to rest the ghosts which keep you in the fetal position, afraid to look up to the light of hope. The One who bears the lamp is holding it high, inviting you to see beyond your loss to his promise. He has important work for you, his work. Even now, he offers the lamp to you. While there is still time, before he begins his homeward journey, ask him. Ask him where he is going. He wants you to know the way.

Clumsy nestlings thrash the air once more from folk oak to poplar
then on spindly branches wobble cockeyed
longing for their womb of tangled bracken
respite from maternal urgings.

Hanging 'gainst the sun she warms them even with her shadow
then in one ascending note of parting
darts to melancholy freedom singing
duty done and duty given.

Merciful Jesus, you were sent to bring solace to the sorrowing. As we thank you for your concern and compassion, we acknowledge another side to your healing ministry: You give us important work to do, a mission which calls us away from self-pity. You charge us to cry out the Good News even before our weeping is over. O Wounded-Healer, bind up our wounds and strengthen us, for we want to be busy with your work.   Amen.

WEDNESDAY OF THE SIXTH WEEK

Paul stood up in the Areopagus and delivered this address: "Men of Athens, I note that in every respect you are scrupulously religious. As I walked around looking at your shrines, I even discovered an altar inscribed, 'To a God Unknown.' Now, what you are thus worshipping in ignorance I intend to make known to you"   (Acts 17:22-23).

When Paul told the best and the brightest of Athens that he was aware of how exacting they were in their worship, he was pulling his punches. The vinegary prosecutor from Tarsus was strewing sugar on the Hill of Mars; these pagan philosophers needed not to know of his exasperation over the many shrines and idols in the city. He bit his tongue and withheld any characterization which would put off potential converts.

In modern parlance, we would diagnose the Athenians as spiritually paranoid. Their gods were out to get them. They toyed with men and women; in the process of the game, certain charges were levied in a kind of divine protection racket. To avoid offending a member of the pantheon not yet named by oracle or theophany, shrines to the entire population of unknown or unrecognized deities were erected on the premise that what you don't know *can* hurt you.

Inordinate fear of heaven's capriciousness did not die with the ancients. A generation after the pastoral enlightenment and theistic personalism of Vatican Council II, too many Catholics and other Christians still think that sacrifice is something one offers in the hope of placating or cajoling an unpredictable, choleric God. Each day the classifieds contain their daily ration of printed prayers, the publication of which is a necessary part of the bargain the petitioner assumes God has approved. Ask a priest to save for you the next "Prayer Never Known to Fail" he picks up from a pew. The forlorn soul caught in this rote devotion must transcribe it nine times and drop each copy in church on separate visits. Only then will it be more powerful than God's opposing will. Then there is the nine-minute novena wherein a desperate follower of an inattentive Christ sets an oven timer for repeated nine minute intervals throughout the day and at the sound of the bell utters a pious formula ensuring that the Father's hand will be stayed or speeded. It is easy to ridicule such unfortunate manifestations of spiritual paranoia, but are the despairing who grasp at these straws any less deserving of understanding than you or I are when we promise alms to the poor or an extra Mass in our time of need?

The eve of the Ascension is a good time to remember precisely who returned to his Father's right hand during the Paschal event. Jesus was not stripped of his humanity when he rose from the dead. To ascend to heaven, it was not necessary for him to shed memories heavy with the suffering inherent in daily life. Although he sits in glory at the right hand of the Almighty, he is no less a human being for his translation. Thus, the desperate need not buy Christ's favor; the sinner, his forgiveness. He came to earth to prove wrong Athenians, Pharisees, Jansenists, all those who see appeasement as the only approach to an aloof, mean-spirited, devious deity.

Jesus was the human face of God. On no page of the New Testament is there a hint of the Messiah as mercenary, no evidence of a quid pro quo. The only requirement for healing was illness, for forgiveness, repentance, for sustenance, hunger. Rather than supposing that Jesus' passage to glory was a flight from compassion, the afflicted Christian should view the Ascension as a process of universalization of all that made the Savior human. He reigns now as king of every heart. The lamp of love is held on high; it illuminates all shadowed souls; its light is freely given.

> Surrounded by her vestals,
> one morning chanced to stroll
> the Oracle of Delphi
> across a terraced knoll.
>
> Entranced by young Apollo,
> she missed her step and fell
> upon the fresh-turned farmland
> provoking her to yell.

> From thence arose the worship
> addressed to ev'ry plow,
> a muddy genuflection
> before the great god Yow!

Compassionate Savior, you are the unbreakable convenant between God and humankind. Despite our failings, you never turn your back on us. We praise you for your constant mercy and seek only to know your love.   Amen.

FEAST OF THE ASCENSION

They were still gazing up into the heavens when two men dressed in white stood beside them. "Men of Galilee," they said, "why do you stand here looking up at the skies? This Jesus who has been taken from you will return, just as you saw him go up into the heavens"   (Acts 1:10-11).

Imagine . . . a fight over a food basket when the observatory had been lit up like a Christmas tree for over a month. Every radio telescope in the reflecting field was now trained on one or the other of the Magellanic Clouds. Chad gave grudging thanks for media hype. If the networks hadn't been running bits on the noise all year, the Directorate would still be grinding out the standing order for a daily sky sweep. The scuttlebutt had it that the President got interested, that he wanted the agency to concentrate on the strange signals. Whatever the cause, the Kepler Klub's decade-long crusade was finally paying off. As a charter member of that loose group of radical astronomers, Chad was at the shop day and night, lucky to get a spare hour at home to kiss Kaitlyn and pat the kids. Now of all times, she wanted him to pack Thanksgiving baskets for the poor. Women! Although he thought himself rather liberated, the taste of unfashionable exasperation was sweet indeed.

On the hill road back to the observatory, he stopped to look down on the field filled with seventy-two of what some anchorman had called "God's ears." Nice touch, but a bit off. He had often seen the hundred-foot hemispheres held together with fragile filaments as ears, but not God's. God wasn't listening for us here, we were listening for . . . well, if not God, something a couple of giant steps better than man. He thought of poor Charlie Rothman who first gathered the group together and confided his secret. The signals they had all ascribed to a source in the Fornax galaxy suddenly seemed to shift to Sculptor, much closer to earth. It took the Kepler Klub seven years to prove there had been a change. Now Charlie was in insurance. The acrimonious debate with Jodrell Bank and Palomar had gotten into the press and someone had to go. That's what Kate had said. "Someone had to go" to the St. Vincent de Paul Center and pack baskets. More and more families were falling through the safety net. He had winced at her jargon as he slammed the door. Safety net. What bleeding-heart liberal had she been listening to?

Two months ago, the source of the noise moved from Sculptor to the Smaller Magellanic Cloud, at least a hundred thousand light years closer. Chad himself leaked the news when it seemed the Directorate would continue by the book. Three weeks of increasingly insistent media questions did the trick. On October 21st, the word came down. Half the field would be focussed on the Smaller Magellanic, the other half on the Greater, even closer to earth. "Will Source Take Another Step?" one of the tabloids blared. A horn blared behind him: Rudy Mason, a loner who had taken over from

Charlie as chief radical. Chad wondered if Rudy's wife was a do-gooder too.

He gunned the coupe, but Rudy's BMW beat him to the shop. The boys were going nuts. The source was moving or had moved. Something was happening just two months from the last fix. Leski and Wiltgen, the resident born-agains, were speechless. Leski punched up one word on his PC: Christmas. Here we go, Chad thought. The Second Coming again. A year ago, Wiltgen heard his preacher tell about the old legend that promised the Second Coming on the anniversary of the first. The others toyed with Wiltgen, then the credulous Leski, coming up with all kinds of pseudo-scientific counter-arguments. Chad got the biggest laugh with the story that the early Church had arbitrarily moved the celebration to replace a pagan feast. Who really knew when Christ was born? Thank God, none of this stuff was overheard by the buzzing reporters. Think of Kate. She'd be packing a basket for the Messiah.

He called around noon. She knew exactly what he'd say, and said it for him. "Something big is on. You won't be home until midnight or maybe later." He knew about what she'd say. He pictured the lost-waif look which came over her when she talked about "my families." She had called the other wives and found that none of the boys from the observatory would be at the Center tonight, the last night before deliveries. Even Leski and Wiltgen had reneged. A few more predictable allusions to what was more important, and she was finished. When they hung up, he figured he would be home long before she tonight. They knew each other very well.

"Men of Galilee, why do you stand here looking up at the skies?" Did Christ go up, or did he go in? Will he issue forth from a spiral nebula or has he been for two thousand years coiled in the double helix of need?

elusive butterfly alight
a miracle with wings
aquiver tensed for instant flight
from dark rememberings
of hope cocooned against the night

uncommon monarch flees to reign
in realms beyond the reach
of logic's net while making plain
the possibility to each
who shares the caterpillar's strain

Lord of glory, you vanished from the sight of the Apostles only to become visible in the lives of your brothers and sisters. May I always strive to see you in the people around me. Call out to me, Lord, in their laughter and sighs. Bring me, through them, to the glory that is yours and yours alone to give.   Amen.

FRIDAY OF THE SIXTH WEEK

Jesus said to his disciples:
"When a woman is in labor she is sad that her time has come. When she has borne her child, she no longer remembers her pain for joy that a man has been born into the world"   (John 16:21).

Happy Birthday Bonnie —

I'm really tired right now and probably not making much sense. The nurse kind of fussed when I asked for some paper and a pencil. She said I should rest but I promised myself that I would put into words what I feel as soon as I could after your arrival. (It was at 6:40 this morning.) When you open this you will be sixteen like I am now. I hope you are having a neat party and won't be where I am now and will wait 'till you're married. But the world is a crazy place and the pressure is awful great. I made a mistake. I almost made two. The second one is what this letter is about.

If you don't know your father's name by the time you read this, you'll never hear it from me. There's nothing wrong with him except he's so immature. I guess I am, too, or I wouldn't be here but he's a seventeen-year-old baby. That sure came out when we told our parents. He cried like a baby at both places he was so scared. I didn't shed a tear. I wasn't worried because there wasn't going to be a baby. There wasn't going to be a you, Bonnie. I already made the appointment before we told Mom and Dad.

I didn't expect much of an argument from either one of them. They both wanted me to go to college. They never liked your father because he quit school and always made fun of our house. Mom (your Grandmother) had just come back from one of her trips to Pleasant Oaks and was on some new medication which made her kind of out of it. But Dad (Grandpa) turned white and asked when was the appointment for. He wasn't mad exactly. He talked very slow and said to ask your father's parents what they thought about it. Well I wasn't going to change my mind no matter what they thought. I wasn't going to be tied down with a baby. And what would the gang say? (Sounds mean but I want you to know all of it.)

His parents, who you'll probably never know, didn't argue. They said it's up to me and him. When he dropped me home Dad was in the living room. Mom was gone to make her daily visit to church. She is really devoted to the Little Flower. Dad came up to my room and sat on the bed. I could see he wasn't taking it the way I figured so I thought this was going to be about what the Church teaches and mortal sin and all that and my immortal soul. They didn't want any more kids after me. They wanted to make sure my brothers and me could go to college and all that. About eight years ago something went wrong. She got pregnant and the doctors told her it would be a very difficult birth at her age. She didn't have it.

They both felt really guilty and went to confession. The priest was really nice and promised that God forgave them. That was enough for him he said but Mom started seeing the baby in her dreams. When your Uncle Ron and Emmy had their first she stopped going to their house. She got so depressed she started going to counselors. I can remember her then. She would cry a lot and take the blame for every little thing that went wrong. This went on for years and I can't tell you what a drag it was when she was bad. Then she went to Pleasant Oaks the first time when I was a freshman. She'd stay there about three weeks a couple times a year. Dad said he thinks she believes God forgave her but she can't forgive herself. She thinks she'll go to heaven but is afraid of what she'll find there — afraid of meeting her baby — afraid of what it will tell her.

Well Bonnie — that's why I changed my mind. I'm not sure I believe in heaven or God after all I've been through. By the time you read this I'll be thirty-two and be more sure. (Hopefully.) But if there is another life I won't be afraid to face you.

Happy Birthday Sweet Sixteen. You were a real pain and made me awful blue. I quit school because of the razzing and morning sickness. If I start again or whatever happens you'll know when you read this. I've still got a chance to do something big. Mom is going to take care of you. Dad says this is the best thing that ever happened to her. Can you believe it? They say two wrongs don't make a right. I came really close to two in a row. Don't you even start, but if you make the first mistake, don't make the second.

Your loving (and tired) Mother

> The wrath of God is often more to be preferred
> than nascent trust betrayed,
> for having heard
> a thousand lies
> He seeks one word
> of true remorse and sighs.
>
> Not so the once defenseless babe at heaven's gate
> whose sharp reproachful cries
> incriminate
> the penitent
> who sealed the fate
> of such an innocent.

Lord of life, Protector of the unborn and Guardian of the aged, inspire our judicial leaders and legislators to heed the cries of the innocent and defenseless. May they come to see, through the witness of caring Christians, that all life is precious and no one life is worth more than any other. Send holy counsel to impressionable youth in times of stress and fear. Amen.

SATURDAY OF THE SIXTH WEEK

> Jesus said to his disciples:
> "I have spoken these things to you
>   in veiled language.
> A time will come when I shall
>   no longer do so,
> but shall tell you about the Father
>   in plain speech"   (John 16:25).

Jesus was the master of the parable, bringing a double purpose to this ancient form of storytelling. To those listeners entrenched in the status quo, these developed similes were a cauterizing flame meant to purify hearts of hypocrisy. The hidebound found the pain unbearable and turned away, nursing their seared psyches. In stories such as that of the good Samaritan and the rich man and Lazarus (Luke 10 and 16, respectively), the elders and high priests recognized themselves as men under indictment. They despised Jesus for his easy rapport with common folk, a relationship constantly nourished by down-to-earth tales about shepherds and nets and wheat and weeds. Perhaps, had he used the sophisticated restraint of courtroom debate, Jesus might have won over more legalists, but the Jew in the pew would have dozed off.

It would be a mistake, however, to assume a symmetry of ends in Jesus' use of parables. There was not that degree of enlightenment sufficient to counterbalance his clearly understood indictment of the scribes and Pharisees. Although he complained about the slowness of his disciples to grasp the simpler aspects of his message, Jesus never attempted to paint a complete picture of the kingdom. It would seem that he chose the parabolic form to introduce a veiled revelation even to those closest to him. His aim was to stimulate rather than explicate, to hold the kingdom just out of reach in order that the sinews of faith might be exercised. In every parable, there came a point where the kingdom and the story coincided, or better, kissed. Except for the homily on the seed and the sower, Jesus stopped short of exactitude, preferring instead to invite his hearers to ponder, to come to insight by means of their own faculties. This teaching method should not surprise, for Jesus' life was itself a parable, a series of events first lived by the Master then told by the faithful, which in its obscure entirety offered an invitation to the sincere of heart. To say that Jesus was the primary Parable is not to deny his historic authencity — Jesus did happen, but to present him as an appeal to faith.

When you hold the lamp of life renewed over a parable, do not expect to see the Alpha and Omega made transparent in every line and lineament. Jesus' simple stories embody his respect for your freedom to choose and your power of imagination. The most important part of any parable is the hearer who puts herself or himself into the scene. The leading men of Israel knew how to listen to parables and found themselves portrayed as knaves and hypocrites. The kiss of truth was for them a slap in the face. The fishermen and farmers, the tax collectors and prostitutes appreciated the form and loved Jesus for the parts he gave them. They may have been slower to understand than the learned, but they gradually saw the outline of a kingdom which included themselves.

That kingdom includes you. Although the day will come when Christ "shall tell you about the Father in plain speech," the kingdom remains indistinct even to the daily Bible reader. It will always be thus, for Jesus meant neither to mesmerize nor to coerce. Yet, little by little, his delicate and respectful invitation will become clearer. In meditation and prayer you will come to know the outline of your story, your personal history of salvation. Each time you earnestly enter a parable will be a moment of fresh insight, be it the balm of consolation or the sting of conscience, but always there shall remain the mystery, always another veil to pierce — until the Day of the Lord when you see the Master Storyteller face to face and hear him in plain speech.

> He set the stage we venture upon,
> proposed the parts, composed the scene.
> The script is blank except for the cues
> to improvise a sketch between
> a shadowed remnant waiting for dawn
> and those who call the darkness light.
> Come, Christian, take your place on these boards;
> the houselights dim, your spot is bright.

Author of the Saving Word, help us to find our roles in the drama of Holy Scripture. In our quiet meditation as in the whirl of everyday life, we seek to immerse ourselves in the action and dialogue of salvation. Although we know not each twist of the plot, we rest easy, for the radiance of the Resurrection reveals a story with a happy ending. Amen.

SEVENTH SUNDAY OF EASTER

> Jesus looked up to heaven and said:
> "I do not pray for them alone.
> I pray also for those who
> will believe in me
> through their word,
> that all may be one
> as you, Father, are in me, and I in you;
> I pray that they may be [one] in us,
> that the world may believe
> that you sent me"   (John 17:20-21).

The sectarian divisions among the followers of Jesus have been called the scandal of Christianity. From the monumental split between Rome and Constantinople in the 11th century through the devastating separations of the Reformation in the 16th, the one body of Christ has been at the mercy of pride, both nationalistic and personal. What the soldiers beneath the cross would not do to the Master's seamless garment, his disciples have accomplished through avarice, fear, and self-righteousness. In our own day, while interdenominational study groups inch their way toward fragile agreements, and leaders such as Pope John Paul II and the Archbishop of Canterbury embrace, their churches and other mainline bodies seethe with homegrown controversy. The willing spirit of reconciliation may be abroad in the land, yet the flesh erupts with internal dissension.

At the end of Jesus' Priestly Prayer, St. John places a plea for unity couched in a style which can seem rather confusing until the reader holds over it the lamp of life renewed. Despite its mystical form, the purpose of the prayer is as practical as the Resurrection. Christ rose from the dead as the firstborn of many brothers and sisters. St. Paul writes: "If Christ was not raised, your faith is worthless. If our hopes in Christ are limited to this life only, we are the most pitiable of men" (1 Corinthians 15:17, 19). As Christ's Resurrection was the necessary precondition for the possibility of eternal life offered to any other human being, so the unity of the Church is the necessary precondition for the possibility that all human beings might learn of this offer. In short, the world cannot grasp the fullness of the promise of eternal life beamed from a Tower of Babel.

If the Church is not the beacon of unity which Christ, the head, meant it to be, the fault must lie in its members. We have not let the communion of the Father and the Son shine through us. When Jesus prays "that all may be one," he asks that we be given the grace to model our relationships with each other on his relationship with his Father, especially in the matter of respecting the other person's dignity and will. All members of the Church have something to contribute; all deserve our openness to and affirmation of their good intentions. When our first reactions to the suggestion or opinion of a fellow believer are those of skepticism or cynicism, apathy or suspicion, we are not living with them or "in them," we are not allowing them to live with us or "in us." It is neither necessary nor fruitful to hold that the variety of talents and experiences of those in the Church must be kneaded into a bland dough; the bread of life is to be savored in a world of many tastes. St. Paul makes clear the miracle of diversity in the Church and the reason for it: We must rely on the manifold gifts of others (See 1 Corinthians 12:1-11). Such mutual dependence flows from the mysterious interdependence of the Father and the Son in the Trinity, a divine dynamism poured out upon the Church by the Holy Spirit.

To the extent that we open ourselves to the Spirit, we share in this dynamic unity of gifts. This sharing enriches not only our spiritual lives, personal and communal; it becomes a most powerful witness to our fractious world. Jesus' Priestly Prayer is finally a benediction upon that world. The Church is for the world. It has no reason for existence without its mission to the world. The promise of eternal life is an offer to all men and women within and outside the Church. In the last analysis, the most damaging aspect of the scandal of sectarian division is not the bloodying of believers but the world's perception of disorder in the body of Christ. If even the separate denominations are houses divided against themselves, what does it profit a searching soul to come in from the outer chaos?

As the Feast of the Holy Spirit approaches, it makes sense to evaluate our openness to the spirit of unity. The unmistakable mandate of Vatican Council II to promote ecumenism among the churches is stymied when we cannot entertain differing opinions in our own Church with courtesy and magnanimity. The strictures imposed on the public airing of doctrinal disputes give wide latitude for speculative scholarship in the academic setting. Most of us, however, need not worry about such high-powered theological argumentation; it is not our ambience. Rather, we would do well to practice more tolerance toward family members and fellow church-workers who do not see things precisely as we do. A confrontational or condescending approach limits our ability to come to mutual understanding. Such understanding is a gift of that Holy Spirit for whose coming we prepare. Heartfelt acceptance of that gift is the first step in healing the differences among ourselves. Only when that healing takes place can we apply what we've learned about the mutual love of the Father and the Son to the world we were sent to baptize.

> The widened eye
> lingers not upon the mote
> marking weakness in a gaze
> contrarious.
>
> A tolerant
> vision more peripheral
> looks beyond the circumstance
> invidious.
>
> This gracious sight
> softly panoramic sees
> seed and soil as well as fruit
> perfidious.
>
> The daunting speck
> set in life's kaleidoscope
> dwindles in the search for views
> harmonious.

Holy Father, you made each of us in your image and likeness. Holy Son, you gave your life for the salvation of us all. Holy Spirit, pour out upon every man and woman the courage to accept one another, the understanding which leads to forgiveness, the wisdom to seek together our common heritage.   Amen.

MONDAY OF THE SEVENTH WEEK

While Apollos was in Corinth, Paul passed through the interior of the country and came to Ephesus. There he found some disciples to whom he put the question, "Did you receive the Holy Spirit when you became believers?" They answered, "We have not so much as heard that there is a Holy Spirit." "Well, how were you baptized?" he persisted. They replied, "With the baptism of John." Paul then explained, "John's baptism was a baptism of repentance. He used to tell the people about the one who would come after him in whom they were to believe — that is, Jesus." When they heard this, they were baptized in the name of the Lord Jesus. As Paul laid his hands on them, the Holy Spirit came down on them and they began to speak in tongues and to utter prophecies   (Acts 19:1-6).

Many contemporary Christians find themselves standing with those Ephesians who told St. Paul that they had not heard of the Holy Spirit. The latter were unaware of the great outpouring of God's Spirit upon the Apostles in Jerusalem on Pentecost and the subsequent conferral of that same Spirit upon many converts resulting in extraordinary gifts and charisms. Their confession of ignorance did not mean they were uninformed about the movement of the spirit of God in the history of his people. It must be supposed they knew of God's creative spirit which brought an ordered world out of chaos, guided the leaders of Israel, and emboldened the prophets. Surely, these disciples at Ephesus were familiar with the universal agency of God's spirit made plain in such prophetic utterances as that of Joel. "I will pour out my spirit on all mankind" (Joel 3:1). In accepting the baptism of John, they had allowed the spirit of repentance to lead them, but the fullness of life in the Holy Spirit was not yet theirs.

Today's Christians know what the Ephesian disciples were yet to learn, that the fullness of the Spirit has been given to the Church starting with Pentecost and extending to and through the present moment. Yet, with that advantage over their ancestors in the faith, many remain listlessly unconvinced, neither having experienced nor expecting the empowerment of Pentecost. The wind and the fire seem to have passed them by in the night or, worse, were never meant for them. Not a few Christians drag themselves through life as disciples only of John the Baptizer, satisfied with repentance, content to avoid the precipice above the abyss. These are the Ten-Commandment-Christians; for every "shall not," they boast a "have not." They will survive the crossing over, but they will not burn with ardor. Should a St. Paul come along to call down the Holy Spirit upon them, they will respectfully decline. Unlike the disciples at Ephesus, they seek no grander revelation, no disconcerting sense of mission. Let the torch be passed to someone else.

This is not the stance with which to begin the last week before the celebration of Pentecost. Treading water isn't enough. Avoiding sin isn't enough. There was a day not too long ago when all our energies were focussed on keeping the soul hermetically sealed lest those ugly black spots appear in the milk bottle. We saw Pentecost as a strange event emerging once a year from the mists of history, the celebration of an exotic myth featuring cowards who suddenly find their voices, fire and wind filling the Upper Room, polyglot preaching producing mass conversion. Since 1967, however, the Charismatic Renewal and other Spirit-centered movements have changed many minds, revealing Pentecost to be a movable feast, a continuing conferral of God's rejuvenating power. Granted, this power can never become familiar; it will always be suffused with the mystery of its source, but it is ours for the asking. Now is the time to take courage and ask. He who makes all things new urges us this week to prepare for what the listless Christian deems unthinkable: new life *now*.

Take stock today of your resistance to life on a higher spiritual plane. Look critically at those comfortable habits of prayer — formula, repetition, posture, and place — which defy the impulse of the Spirit of renewal. Look, too, at your attitudes toward others, the safe routines of greeting, conversing, relating which protect you from the spontaneity of life in the Spirit. Be at least as wise as the Ephesian disciples who discovered something was missing and bowed their heads to the hands of St. Paul, to that touch trembling with energy.

> Christopher Columbus,
> Marconi, Faraday,
> Thomas Alva Edison,
> les deux Montgolfiers
> Ferdinand Magellan,
> the Curies, she and he,
> Lou and Augie Lumiere,
> Sam Morse, indeed, F.B.,
> Einstein, Clark and Lewis,
> de Forest, Fulton, Watt,

Huxleys two, Copernicus,
Joe Priestly, Robert Scott,
Goddard, Benjy Franklin,
wherever they may dwell
greet each new arrival with
a common truth to tell:
Praise you not our insight
for wonder was our guide;
questing spirits enter first
the door that's opened wide.

Spirit of God, open our hearts to the depth of your love, our minds to the breadth of your wisdom, our lives to the fullness of your creative power. Renew in us each day the baptism of Jesus Christ, our Lord. Amen.

TUESDAY OF THE SEVENTH WEEK

But now, as you see, I am on my way to Jerusalem, compelled by the Spirit and not knowing what will happen to me there — except that the Holy Spirit has been warning me from city to city that chains and hardships await me. I put no value on my life if only I can finish my race and complete the service to which I have been assigned by the Lord Jesus, bearing witness to the Gospel of God's grace (Acts 20:22-24).

A city's importance is measured by the size of the plane which flies there. Harry made a mental note to resurrect his belief in St. Christopher as the vintage Beechcraft bounced to a stop. He was sure that fear had wrung every drop of sweat out of him as the nonchalant pilot threaded the mountain passes, certain, that is, until he popped the passenger door and chafed his pores on the wall of equatorial heat. The inside of his cassock became an instant sauna. Sauna . . . he drifted back to Detroit, to the seminary's exercise room. A doctorate in Scripture, four years as head of the department, an eye on the Rector's office — then the call from Father Superior. Jumpin' Jack Baumgartner was building a vocational school in a South American rain forest and needed a director. Would he go? "No," Harry said. Two days later he got his letter.

A Brother Arnoldo met him with the news that the Jeep heaving next to the hanger had broken something he couldn't understand in Spanish. Padre Jack was coming in *el camion*. Harry dropped his bag under a resinous tree and sat down, careful not to lean back against the glistening trunk. It had taken two weeks of home leave and a retreat to produce a grudging resignation. Brotherly counsel was not helpful; the voices of his friends back from mission still echoed. Jack Baumgartner was nuts, thought he was the Messiah of the jungle, proposed to build a school thirty miles from the nearest town to show solidarity with the forest people. If he wasn't the Superior's uncle, he would be weeding the garden at the Motherhouse.

There was another voice, too, a silent whisper at the end of every agonizing meditation. It was vaguely reminiscent of a John Wayne movie he and his fellow novices had laughed at back at St. Mary's. "This is what you signed up for: Hell on the equator." He remembered his youthful zeal pulsing beneath the obligatory cynicism, and how his nineteen-year old heart would nearly burst when the veterans returned to tell their annual horror stories of life on mission. Soon after ordination, though, heroism gave way to the satisfaction of studying, then teaching St. Luke, and after eight years, well, any man, priest or not, can get awfully comfortable at thirty-six. Excellent methodology, sensitive liturgist, good administrator; the evaluations began to get boring. But, oh, to be bored like that this steamy afternoon.

Under the dripping leaves, he prayed. Not for a telegram calling him back. Not even that by some miracle Jack Baumgartner had been suddenly struck sane. He prayed that he might stop hearing the insistent reminders. He was here, wasn't he? If God wanted him to do a good work, why the constant allusions to the trial? Wasn't it enough that he had come on his own power, not dragged kicking and screaming, not petitioning for a reconsideration? Why this preview of the gauntlet? He was going to make the run. . . . The sharp backfire of a truck jerked him against the gluey tree. Jumpin' Jack Baumgartner had one hand on the steering wheel, the other brandishing a battered roll of blueprints. *"Bienvenido!* Harry. Welcome to God's country."

Today's reading from the Acts of the Apostles reveals that St. Paul was a bit premature in bidding the Ephesians farewell; he would be back one more time. He was quite correct, however, in confessing the paradox of mission. The compelling word of the Holy Spirit not only sends out, it also cautions, forewarns, anticipates the way of suffering. Like Father Harry, all who set out to do God's work hear sooner or later a harsher inflection in the call to action. The Spirit of Truth will not be bound by romantic dreams of steely courage and golden accomplishment. It is, after all, Christ's own Spirit which summons men and women to ministry, the Spirit of the Suffering Servant who warned his disciples that trial must precede triumph.

As you prepare to open your heart to the outpouring of the Spirit on Pentecost, remember that you are asking for nothing less than the truth. Tongues of fire, rushing wind, speaking in tongues, mass conversions are marginal phenomena, exciting but unnecessary confirmations of indwelling grace, that strength of soul required for your particular mission. Few may know these wonders, but all are empowered, all are sent. One thing only is required: realism, a clear light illuminating the finish line *and* the rocky track. This, too, is the lamp of life renewed, the Spirit of the Risen Christ who conquered death, but not before he suffered death. "The Holy Spirit has been warning me from city to city that chains and hardships await me." Whether your destination is Jerusalem, a tropical rain forest, or a friend straying from the faith, the way is that of witness, and witness has its price.

> So many race the darkness
> to gain a prize unknown;
> they stumble on deceptive paths
> and curse each upturned stone.
>
> To those more blest is given
> the Spirit's constant light;
> it does not smooth the rocky road
> but sets their course aright.

Spirit of Truth, let not our fear of adversity blind us to our mission. We accept our role in renewing the face of the earth, but rely on your guidance and protection. Be the light of our lives as we follow the way of the Lord. Amen.

WEDNESDAY OF THE SEVENTH WEEK

> Jesus looked up to heaven and said:
> "Consecrate them by means of truth —
> 'Your word is truth.'
> As you have sent me into the world,
> so I have sent them into the world,
> I consecrate myself for their sakes now,
> that they may be consecrated in truth"
> (John 17:17-19).

The power lunch: Twelve division managers stand quietly around the great mahogany table in the Founder's Dining Room on the 37th floor. They smile broadly when the Chief Executive Officer enters, then take their seats after him. During the two hours of chicken bouillon, lettuce wedge with oil and vinegar, braised veal, four-bean pilaf, bread sticks, and Chablis, a sales program will be funded, a production line retooled, three regional directors will be transferred, a pricing strategy confirmed, and 235 workers laid off. By the time the compote is served, each of the managers in his or her own way will have congratulated the C. E. O. for his courage in approving the tough decisions necessary to keep Amalgamated competitive. One, the newest member of the team, trading on his boyish charm, will stand and say: "J. C., you have covered yourself with glory today."

Power lunches, power plays, power politics, power brokers, power grabs: Buzzwords betray our fascination with control as we seek to take into our own hands the instruments and strategies which determine the destinies of others. Today's hero is the person who charts his or her own course and devil take the hindmost. The theme song of the age is "I Did It My Way." Regrets? We may have a few, but the mistakes were our own and they made the victories that much sweeter. Satisfaction flows from self-direction, independent decisions, manipulation of resource and circumstance. To mold the world into our own image and likeness is to cover ourselves with glory.

Twelve men reclined at table in a room one flight up to hear their Master describe a different kind of power, that of sacrifice, the dedication of self to a greater good. Jesus called upon his heavenly Father to set these disciples aside, to commission them to selflessness, to consecrate them to the truth. Only he knew the whole truth, that glory lies in the consecration itself. The men who surrounded him had given ample proof of their fascination with the final triumph; to them the present struggle was a half-life, a time for shallow breathing until power fell into their hands. They did not want to hear that the outcome was still in doubt, that in consecrating himself to the truth, Jesus was putting his fate into the hands of men. For the last time, Jesus tried to make it clear to those closest to him that he would go first into the fearsome night so they might have a light to guide them when they stepped into the darkness. The glory of his sacrifice would illuminate their way.

Those who consecrate themselves to the way of Christ, find that glory is already theirs. Each of us can remember times when anxiety over our own well-being melted in the presence of another's peril. It may have been an act of heroism or simply companionship given to a desperate friend. Our worries faded as we brought the power of God to bear on a dismal situation. Whether or not our mission was ultimately successful, the experience of being a channel of healing grace made us glow with the Lord's own strength as it coursed through our soul. That flow of compassion, that illuminating love was the glory of which Jesus spoke in his Priestly Prayer. We were consecrated, dedicated, set aside to do God's will in the moment of someone else's pain. We shared the glory that Jesus knew in the garden of Gethsemane when he said: "Not my will but yours be done." We let God's will be done in us and entered if only for a time his glorious realm as cooperators in the healing of his people.

Check your personal definition of power and glory. If too often the former means manipulation of others and the latter means self-aggrandizement, you need to read again Jesus' Priestly Prayer in the seventeenth chapter of John's Gospel. There, power is the decision to dedicate one's self to the will of God and glory is the doing of God's will. It makes sense, doesn't it? Who is more powerful than he who lets God's creative love flow through his soul? Who is more glorious than she who radiates that love?

> Check your titles at the door,
> shed that honored name.
> Servants had you by the score?
> Here you face the same
> questions as the chambermaid
> free from her travail.
> Wealth and power are not weighed
> on the Master's scale.

> Did you ever make a lap
> for an orphaned child?
> When the footman dropped your wrap,
> was your answer mild?
> Did you think that pride of place
> would survive the end?
> Upstairs, downstairs, muslin, lace
> this fine day must blend.

Liege and lackey, knight and knave
side by side now stand
telling of the love they gave
at the Lord's command:
Every Christmas I sent down
sovereigns to my staff.
I, to chase a beggar's frown,
broke my bread in half.

God of power and might, free me from self-concern so that I may be more sensitive to the needs of others. In dedicating myself to your will, I ask for the gift of abundant love; may it fill this earthen vessel and flow out upon your children, my anguished brothers and sisters. For their sakes, consecrate me in compassion. Amen.

THURSDAY OF THE SEVENTH WEEK

I bless the Lord who counsels me;
> even in the night my heart exhorts me.

I set the Lord ever before me;
> with him at my right hand
>> I shall not be disturbed   (Psalm 16:7-8).

Perhaps too often in these pages the Holy Spirit has been described as an electrifying presence entering the lethargic soul to induce a kind of holy havoc, urging, pressing, challenging, shaming, stimulating. It is difficult to characterize the mutual love of the Father and the Son as anything but explosive, radiant, salvific energy. The Paraclete promised by Christ is most easily seen as a dervish of advocacy, a super-conductor of missionary zeal.

Fascination with the dynamism of the Holy Spirit is understandable, but prayerful Christians know another side of the Third Person of the Trinity. After all, the guidance of the Church and its members requires more than an occasional kick in the pants. The faithful live from day to day rather than from glory to glory. The valleys far outnumber the peaks. It is in the quiet valleys of the recollected soul that the seven gentle gifts of the Holy Spirit are appreciated most.

Wisdom comes to us in the silent tension of decision-making. Though the future is cloudy, a choice must be made today. Wisdom reminds us that God is our goal and our guide. It is a lamp which lights the path just into tomorrow. The day after tomorrow, we shall seek wisdom again.

Understanding complements wisdom by keeping our final destination in the forefront of our minds. Our pilgrimage is not made less arduous, but we are convinced that the journey is worthwhile. Understanding helps us put everyday struggles in proper perspective; they pale in comparison to the promise of eternal life.

Counsel assures us that God wants to hear our prayers. In the sometimes strident debates over the best methods of communication with the divine, counsel says that it doesn't make any difference. God strains to catch our every word and can decipher even the most agitated jumble of petition and praise. The gift of counsel is the gift of innocence in prayer.

Fortitude is the strength needed to keep on keeping on in a world which seems to delight in tripping up the sincere Christian. It counters the spiritual exhaustion which overcomes the believer striving to lead a moral life in an amoral society. Fortitude is the second wind of the soul.

Knowledge orders the elements of faith; it brings common sense to matters of doctrine and creed. Doubts are part of everyone's spiritual journey; knowledge points to the far horizon, prevents uncertainties about details from becoming massive roadblocks to fruitful communion with God. Molehills remain molehills when the gift of knowledge is invoked.

Piety is not folded hands and custody of the eyes. It is confidence that God loves us even when our hands flutter up and our eyes wander. It is a gift wrapped in peace, the peace which comes only to those who strive to do God's will even though they often fail. The pious person is sure that God's way is the best way.

Fear of the Lord means respect for the God who emptied himself to become one of us. It is not the dread exemplified by Dorothy and her friends as they shivered before the Wizard of Oz. We need not fear God-made-flesh; he is to be praised precisely because of his Incarnation. This gift helps us honor the One who affirmed our worth by becoming one of us.

The Holy Spirit is love, at once dynamic and serene, energetic and peaceful. While the gifts of the Spirit should result in a more active ministry, they must first be accepted in the silence of meditation. They are yours for the asking, available at your favorite prayer-place.

> Wisdom makes the righteous choice
> Understanding lights the way
> Counsel hears the prayerful voice
> Fortitude keeps sin at bay
> Knowledge anchors faith in flight
> Piety conforms the will
> Fear of God respects his might
> Seven gifts our hearts to fill

Serene Spirit of Love, fill our hearts with your seven holy gifts. Let us rest for a moment in your tender affection; then, refreshed by this blessed communion, we shall arise to share your generosity with our waiting world. Amen.

FRIDAY OF THE SEVENTH WEEK

> When [Jesus manifested himself to his disciples and] they had eaten their meal, he said to Simon Peter, "Simon, son of John, do you love me more than these?" "Yes, Lord," Peter said, "you know that I love you." At which Jesus said, "Feed my lambs"   (John 21:15).

A valid question, this. "Do you love me?" A question put to a man who tried to dissuade Jesus from his mission of salvation through suffering (Mark 8:32), who selfishly sought an honored place in the kingdom (Mark 10:41), who denied three times he even knew Jesus (Mark 14:66-72), who was probably absent from the crucifixion (John 19:25-27), and who returned to his former occupation after the death and post-Resurrection appearances of his Master (John 21:1-3). John's Gospel is a bit too generous in reporting Peter's answer; his reply might better be phrased: "Yes, Lord, and you know how little I have loved you." Jesus' question must have forced Peter to acknowledge the weakness of his commitment; after his flight from Jerusalem to the sea of Tiberias, he could hardly boast that he loved Jesus "more than these" other disciples. Thus, the surprise which surely followed Jesus' next statement: "Feed my lambs."

Today's Scripture passage makes it clear that Jesus uses vessels of clay to bear his healing balm to the world. He does not require perfection in his messengers, only willing hearts which know their own fragility. There is a legend based on Matthew 26:75 which claims the tears Peter shed after his third denial of Jesus in the high priest's courtyard were so bitter that they burned permanent scars into his cheeks. Certainly, shame over his cowardice scarred his soul so that his conscience could not permit a confident avowal of love at the sea of Tiberias. He knew that Jesus saw how inconstant was his commitment. And yet, this grand commission, this reaffirmation of his primacy over others who may have been more loyal: "Feed my lambs."

Once again, Jesus made clear the paradox of discipleship. It was precisely those bitter tears and that implicit admission of failure which moved Jesus to renew his trust in Peter. It was precisely in this setting, the end of a frustrating night of labor on the sea, that Jesus wanted Peter to begin his mission. Until the big fisherman admitted his weakness, he could not wholeheartedly turn to Christ for empowerment. Until he returned to the world of work where a livelihood must be wrested from nature, this power could not be fruitfully manifested. Peter and his comrades would discover the retreat to their former vocations to be the beginning of the involvement of the Spirit in the push and shove of human affairs, and that Christ's forgiveness and healing of their own souls was the seed of the Good News they would proclaim to all nations.

We cannot open ourselves to the power of Christ's Holy Spirit unless we face our failures. If Jesus wanted crystal decanters as vessels of salvation, he would have commanded his angels to pour out his grace from on high. Instead, he calls Peter and you and me to walk among our brothers and sisters ministering his mercy. We are to be only what we are, fragile and unfinished, so that others will not recoil from haughty perfection but be drawn to the radiance of his love

Friday of the Seventh Week

streaming from earthen vessels. The warmth of divine compassion does not flow down upon the world from the mountaintop. It is spread from person to person at the level of human concourse. We are not to leave the shore of Tiberias, the factory, the office, the schoolyard; rather, we are to bear the lamp in the shadows of the daily struggle where our brothers and sisters cry out for more light.

Today, give thanks for the paradox of discipleship. The commissioning of Peter, that oh, so human being, is Christ's call to each of us to do our most important work right where we are. In our weakness, we are to proclaim the Father's strength to save. In our shame, we are to assure the sinner of Christ's forgiveness. In our wandering, we are to share our faith in the guidance of the Holy Spirit.

> Flawless the diamond of our dreams
> each facet an accusation
> reflecting a base gradation
> the imperfection of our schemes.
>
> Shamed by the foibles mirrored there
> we practice dissimulation
> preferring to resignation
> an artfully insouciant air.
>
> Truth lingers just behind our eyes
> belying impersonation
> recalling the lowly station
> of rhinestones notwithstanding guise.
>
> Better to polish humble glass
> in hopeful anticipation
> of God's loving invitation
> to give this world a touch of class.

Lord Jesus, God and man, you took our flesh that we might see in you our value and our destiny. We seek not to escape the world you consecrated by your coming; rather, we dedicate ourselves to the ministry of healing and renewal. Pour out your Holy Spirit to strengthen our commitment. Amen.

SATURDAY OF THE SEVENTH WEEK

As Peter followed Jesus, he turned around and noticed that the disciple whom Jesus loved was following (the one who had leaned against Jesus' chest during the supper and said, "Lord, which one will hand you over?"). Seeing him, Peter was prompted to ask Jesus, "But Lord, what about him?" "Suppose I want him to stay until I come," Jesus replied, "how does that concern you? Your business is to follow me" (John 21:20-22).

There was a widespread belief in the primitive Christian community that the Second Coming of Christ was imminent. Among the sources of this sometimes fevered anticipation (See Paul's cautionary Letters to the Thessalonians) were some rather ambiguous sayings of Jesus himself including his statement to Peter in today's Scripture passage. Long before the final composition of John's Gospel, there was an oral tradition given wide currency that Jesus in one of his post-Resurrection appearances had told Peter that John, the beloved disciple, would not die "until I come," that is, until Jesus returned to earth as judge of the living and the dead. Although the author of the Fourth Gospel takes pains to refute this assumption — "Jesus never told him . . . that the disciple was not going to die" (John 21:23), for perhaps fifty years after the Ascension the opposing view enjoyed acceptance. Not unexpectedly, as the news of the death of various Apostles filtered back to the young Church over the years, the longevity of the beloved disciple attracted increasing interest. Then came the day when John's death was reported. Christ had not returned. Christians hoping to be swept up to heaven with the triumphant King had a big problem.

Although St. Paul among others had been quite consistent in stressing the uncertainty of the time of Christ's return, some of those convinced of the immediacy of the rapture became disillusioned. The resultant loss of fervor triggered a gradual drift from practice and belief. Today, we would call it a crisis of faith.

Many contemporary Christians are experiencing a similar crisis. After two thousand years of waiting, we are more composed concerning the arrival of the final day, but those twenty centuries are important when we weigh our hopes for human progress against the seeming disintegration of modern life. To put it bluntly: If Christ came to save the world way back then, why are things still in such a mess? Why was the wholesale bloodletting of the wars of the Middle Ages repeated twice in our own century? Why is bubonic plague being mirrored in mass starvation in the sub-Sahara or in the 100% death rate of AIDS? Why does the betrayal of Jesus arise anew in our own day in the assassinations of prominent leaders? Why, in short, are we committing the same sins and falling victim to the same disasters as those which bedeviled and crushed our ancestors? Faith is still taking a beating. Believers still fall away. Could the dirty little secret of human existence be that it is a never-ending crisis from which there is no rescue?

God sends his Holy Spirit to answer, to teach us the lesson directed to the disillusioned in the newborn Church, namely, that crisis has another side called opportunity. The early Christians who opened themselves to the promptings of the Spirit were steadied in their wavering faith by a revaluation of their mission. The postponement of Christ's return forced them to broaden their horizons. No longer were they to concentrate on the exclusivity of salvation; they gradually came to see that the Lord's promises were meant for all men and women. The whole world was to hear the Good News; those who remained steadfast were to be given time to carry the message to the ends of the earth. Crises would not be abolished; henceforth, they would become opportunities for those who could grasp them, opportunities to make straight the way of the Lord.

In our day, this work of the Holy Spirit continues. When we open our hearts to the Spirit's urgings, we are accepting the power to transform that part of the world for which we are responsible. Opening our hearts means accepting the responsibility for turning crises into opportunities. The delay of the Second Coming provides at least one more chance to heal the sick and comfort the bereaved. The disillusion of our age is the fertile ground for those who sow seeds of hope.

As you prepare to celebrate the pouring out of the Holy Spirit tomorrow, there is no need to pray for fertile ground. There is enough disappointment and heartbreak, illness and calamity in our wounded world to keep God's messengers busy for a million lifetimes. Pray instead for the courage to accept the responsibility for renewal, for the willingness to bear the lamp in the darkness, for the optimism which gives witness to your steadfast belief that Christ is present here and now in his Holy Spirit. Pray for all this, then step out the door.

Like a thief	Let us steal
in the night	one more day
comes the Lord	thief from thief
with his might.	while we may.

Urgent Spirit, help us seize the day. Open our hearts and our horizons to the goodness which we and our world long to know. We seek not merely to await the King's coming but to hasten it, to proclaim his presence now among his wayward subjects.   Amen.

PENTECOST

In the beginning, when God created the heavens and the earth, the earth was a formless wasteland, and darkness covered the abyss, while a mighty wind swept over the waters   (Genesis 1:1-2).

At the sight of the Lord the disciples rejoiced.
    "As the Father has sent me,
    so I send you."
Then he breathed on them and said:
    "Receive the Holy Spirit"   (John 20:20-22).

When the day of Pentecost came it found them gathered in one place. Suddenly from up in the sky there came a noise like a strong, driving wind which was heard all through the house where they were seated. Tongues as of fire appeared, which parted and came to rest on each of them. All were filled with the Holy Spirit. They began to express themselves in foreign tongues and make bold proclamation as the Spirit prompted them   (Acts 2:1-4).

In the second chapter of the Acts of the Apostles, the new creation begins fittingly enough with the wind. The same spirit which God breathed upon the formless mass of the newborn earth to separate the dry land from the sea whirls upon Jerusalem, snapping the tattered curtain of the Temple, unfurling the stiffened scroll of the Torah, sweeping from Golgotha the dust of despair. Luke's account of a Pentecost fifty days after Easter crackles with energy: Flames dance in the Upper Room driving erstwhile cowards to brave proclamation in the streets; three thousand hear the Good News in their own languages; a Church is born in spectacle and wonder.

Just as we marvel at the might of the Creator in fashioning the world at its beginning, so we stand in amazement at the birth pangs of the Church. But astonishment and awe are fleeting feelings. Abiding commitment springs from the serene soul. Our age has seen too much of the spectacular; we seek the Church and its animating Spirit on a more intimate level, in a more enduring experience.

The scene described in the twentieth chapter of the Gospel according to John is less daunting. No fire, no wind, no bold proclamation; instead, a breath, quiet and mild yet unmistakably reminiscent of the last wrenching act on Calvary. This is fitting, too, for he who commended his spirit to the Father now commits his Spirit to the first of those who would make up the new people of God. Here, too, a Church is born, an assembly of individuals each of whom must be imbued with the yearning for unity and the power to accomplish it.

In the book of Genesis, the spirit which brooded over the waters is the same spirit which God breathed into Adam's nostrils. Our first parents would beget God's assembly if they kept his law. They didn't obey, nor did their sons and daughters through the ages. One Friday afternoon, they went too far. It was time for a second creation, for a renewed people who would allow God to breathe upon them again. "Receive the Holy Spirit," he said in his Son. So quiet was that gathering in the Upper Room, so intimate; God stood once more in the Garden sharing his spirit with his children.

We, who breath the spirit of God, are Adam and Eve in the modern world. With the example of the Apostles to guide us, we are to people the new Church, we are to beget sons and daughters in the Lord. It is a commission which does not require spectacle or surprise. The world was created by the power of God and re-created by the Passion, Death, and Resurrection of Christ. These wonders are never to be repeated. But the slow and steady breathing of our first parents as they tasted divine love, the quiet inspiration which came over the Apostles as they inhaled the peaceful power of Christ are to happen anew in us each day, each ordinary hour of the life of the world. "Receive the Holy Spirit," Jesus says to us at the moment of sorrow or joy, turmoil or serenity, at every moment which he has chosen to be his own. For his followers, for us, this is the only real time; there are no other moments.

At this moment on the fiftieth day of our journey through light and darkness, we are grateful that the breath of Christ is mild enough to caress rather than convulse the flame of faith. Those who sought a mighty wind courted danger. Faith is fragile; spectacle and prodigy may make it dance, but the risk is great. If the lamp of life is to give light to live by, it must burn with a steady flame. "Then he breathed on them" a gentle Spirit, a breath that would neither die nor cause to die.

At this moment, we recognize our place in that new creation which began to unfold on Easter Sunday. For seven weeks, we have submitted the flame of faith to the Holy Spirit's peaceful urgings. For seven weeks, that flame has grown stronger and brighter. Dark places have been illuminated, fears dispelled, sin forgiven, hope burnished. The path ahead is clearer, more inviting in spite of dangers we know lie over the next hill. The Spirit nourishes the light in our lamp, gives itself to the flame. The Spirit is a promise, the flame a promise fulfilled. The gentle breath of Jesus will never again be smothered; the lamp of life need never be extinguished if we hold it up to the Lord. If we raise it high in confidence, it will become a beacon drawing forth those who wander in the shadows.

Someone was wandering in the shadows that night, missing when Jesus breathed on his Apostles. For another week, Thomas would doubt that the Master had returned, would demand material proof of his rising. There are many Thomases among us, men and women whose faith flickers weakly. They, too, need to know the promise, need to see the flame strong and constant in the Church. Our lamp cannot be hidden under the bushel basket of self-protection. We must be confident enough to expose our faith to the unfriendly winds of the world, certain enough of the Spirit's gentle power to attract the doubters to this new creation. As Thomas came finally to acknowledge "My Lord and my God," so must these find the promise and its fulfillment in the bright assembly of believers.

This Pentecost Day, be assured that the Spirit moves in the Church, quietly, gently. If you seek it in the unusual or the extraordinary, you will be frustrated. It is as natural as breathing in and breathing out. It is Christ breathing upon your world. Hold the lamp high; let the flame be nourished; let your light shine before all.

Pentecost

Hear, my people, hear
this once despairing remnant
ransomed now from fear
facing the motley throng
urging on each a song
of His rebirth
Who gently gathers
all the lost of earth.

Sing, my people, sing!
In multitongued ensemble
let your voices ring
piercing the toneless dirge
quelling the ancient urge
to sigh resigned
against the howling
of the hopeless mind.

Soft, my people, soft.
Think not the risen Jesus
mounts a throne aloft
welcoming anthems hurled
judging a distant world
instead he dwells
in hearts intoning
tunes the Spirit tells.

Sing, my people, sing!
Above the empty gibbet
now the Dove takes wing
rising from stony nest
crooning at love's behest
a hymn of praise
the harmonizing
grace of fifty days.

Come, Spirit of Life, live in your Church. Nourish the flame of faith the world longs to see. Make of us each a light renewed, a promise fulfilled, a beacon to guide those who search for safe haven. Singing the music of the blest, we lift the lamp on high.   Amen.

A FINAL WORD

What began in the early spring with a faint glimmer of hope escaping from a chink in a massive burial stone has become a flood of life-giving light. Fifty days ago, the possibility of anyone's victory over death was no more than a flickering flame. Now, thanks to the nurturing breath of the Holy Spirit, that flame has been fanned into a torch for the world, a beacon whose beams stream from pole to pole, warming hearts and enlightening the souls of God's people everywhere. The sun itself hastily readies its summer smile as if, caught unaware by the strength of this burgeoning light, it must contend with a serious rival. The sun will lose, just as any beam kindled by man or nature will pale against the radiance of God's saving love reborn.

And yet. . . . There will be dreary days in the future. Summer brings its storms, days when the clouds hang so low that the lamp of life will be all but obscured. Loneliness, partings, anxiety threaten to enshroud the most hopeful hearts. With barely a moment's notice, laborers in the vineyard can be chilled by the cold rain of swiftly-moving disappointment. They know that the sun shines above the storm, but it seems not to shine for them; they shiver with the suspicion of betrayal.

These pages were meant to bring reassurance of the power and permanency of God's love aglow in the radiance of the Resurrection. It is that certainty which will carry us through the fickle weather ahead. Casting eyes of faith toward leaden skies, we shall again pierce the veils of mist to behold the lamp of life. We have rejoiced in that light for seven weeks; it has been at one and the same time the creative power of the Father's love, the saving grace flowing from Christ's sacrifice, and the insistent invitation of the Holy Spirit to brotherhood and sisterhood. Our belief has been our joy, namely, that the light will always be there for us and for all who seek it with sincere hearts. If some would call this blind faith, so be it. Convinced Christians are prepared to be, yes, yearn to be blinded by this light.

As Peter, James, and John fell down in awe at the radiant transfiguration of their Master on Mt. Tabor, so we find too dazzling the creation of the world from nothing, the assumption of our flesh by the Second Person of the Trinity, his triumph over death, the conversion of three thousand by once-stuttering shepherds and fishermen, the flowering of a world-wide Church built on outcasts and self-confessed sinners. It is too much; the light is too bright. We shield our eyes from this brilliance. But the truth has registered, the warmth of love will be remembered, the light has been captured in the retinae of our souls. Even when we close our eyes, the gleam of glory will be there. Blind faith? Better to call it reality observed with the inner eye. We know what we have seen. It has become part of our very being, there to be recalled when darkness threatens hope. It is clarity and warmth for the dreariest day. It is the lamp of life renewed.

If you have been blessed with a few minutes of prayerful meditation each day during the Easter Season, give thanks for the light which has come into your life. Give thanks by heeding the call to be a lamp-bearer. Each of your prayers, no matter how solitary, no matter how personal, contained a plea for the world's enlightenment, for those of

God's children who have yet to be convinced that the glory has not faded. Do not give up your habit of prayer just because Pentecost has passed. Even the wavering flame of your most distracted meditations is like the sun in the darkness of another's doubting soul. Now, the gift of illumination which you seek and receive is to be given to others. Let the Spirit of Pentecost draw you into the obscure streets as it did the Apostles. In many parts of your own world, the sun has barely risen. To you, the stumbling cry, "More light!" To you, the Spirit calls, "Take up the Lamp!"

> In a plan of surpassing beauty the Creator of the universe decreed the renewal of all things in Christ. In his design for restoring human nature to its original condition, he gave a promise that he would pour out on it the Holy Spirit along with his other gifts, for otherwise our nature could not enter once more into the peaceful and secure possession of those gifts. He gave this promise when he said: *In those days*, that is, the days of the Savior, *I will pour out a share of my Spirit on all mankind* (Joel 3:1).
>
> St. Cyril of Alexandria

You have been enlightened with the wisdom of the Holy Spirit, strengthened with the same trust manifested by the Savior in his suffering, and reformed by the Father's creative love. Thus blessed, go now bearing the lamp of new life to a world waiting in the shadows.